WE MOVE TONIGHT

The Making of the Grenada Revolution

Joseph Ewart Layne

GRMF

Grenada Revolution Memorial Foundation

Copyright © 2014 by Joseph Ewart Layne

All rights reserved.

ISBN-13: 978-1492724582
ISBN-10: 1492724580

DEDICATION

To

My darling daughter, Tania

Inspiration

…people anywhere being inclined
and having the power have the right to rise up
and shake off the existing government
and form a new one that suits them better.
This is a most valuable, a most sacred right
 – a right which, we hope and believe,
is to liberate the world.

Abraham Lincoln

Freedom Hill

Oh what a night a lovely night
It's Revolution eve
Grenada looks as radiant
As she has ever been
There lies beautiful Grand Anse Beach
Just resting at its peace
Its silver sand
Like eyes
Reflect
The beauty of the land

A beauty which inspires men
To endear themselves to thee
And risk their lives in struggle
To ensure that you are free

Your smile is a romantic breeze
That breeze is cool and fresh
It soothes the nerves
Caresses the body
And lays the mind to rest

There is message in your breath
It whispers to the ear
Your heroes from their graves declare
" Our spirits are all near"

Tonight atop of Freedom Hill
Their words come loud and clear
A grouping of your noble sons
Are gathered there to hear

Workers
Farmers
Teachers
Students

And lawyers too
Tonight they vow to take a stand
To free thee
Motherland

The moon is bright never so quite
The sky is full of stars
Mother Nature
Extends her light
To guide our noble fight

That moon with all its splendour
Carries the hope of dawn
The centuries dream of thee
Homeland
Preparing to be born

Like Fedon and the slaves
Whose spirits we invoke
The galaxies are out in force
In show of their support.

And as I look up yonder
I see dark waning to light
On top of Freedom Hill tonight
The moon is extra bright

At cockcrow's hour
Like a fireball
The sun flashes a ray
In True Blue Green Beast drop their guns
In shock they wake and run

Like owls they flee the ray of light
It was such a wondrous sight
A long dark night passes away
And suddenly it's bright!

Joseph Ewart Layne, 1987

ACKNOWLEDGEMENTS

I wish to acknowledge the assistance of all sixteen of my colleagues who were imprisoned with me. But special appreciation to Leon "Bogo" Cornwall, Bernard Coard, John "Chalky" Ventour, Lester Redhead and Christopher Stroude. Their invaluable assistance and encouragement have made this book a reality.

I express special appreciation to the person who in 1988 smuggled this book out of prison. You know yourself.

Appreciation to my brother, Raymond, who in 1988 on his own initiative ensured that the handwritten manuscript was typed up and thereby preserved.

I acknowledge all those who have encouraged me to publish the book. I especially acknowledge Ralston Adams, deceased, who initially edited the book and Liam Martin who did a further editing in 2013. Liam also gave invaluable advice on the structure of the book, and was decisive in organizing it for publication.

Sincere appreciation to my parents and all my siblings, and a network of very dear friends, whose love and selfless support sustained me through my long prison ordeal. At the risk of omitting some friends who should be mentioned, I must specially mention Karen my darling wife, Andre, Swallow and Ashley.

I especially remember my dear friend and brother, Dr. David Lambert, one of the heroes of the story of this book, who, in January 2010, shortly after I was released from prison, succumbed to cancer.

Finally, to pay homage to all the persons who made the story of this book a reality, I have made a gift of the copyright to the Grenada Revolution Memorial Foundation Inc. (GRMF). GRMF is a non-profit corporation whose main objective is to preserve the memory of the Grenada Revolution. As such all profits from the sale of the book and distribution of other rights connected thereto will go to GRMF.

Table of Contents

Introduction

An explosion took place in the Caribbean on March 13, 1979. A 'Grenade' detonated! Revolution erupted in the then unknown island of Grenada. So earth-shattering was its effect that it shook the entire Caribbean Region and the Americas. So loud was the explosion that it was heard in every corner of the globe.

In the US, President Carter convened a meeting of his National Security Council. The CIA scrambled to gather information on the Caribbean and more specifically on Grenada. For many years the CIA had shown benign neglect for the English-speaking Caribbean; now suddenly, the region was elevated to the status of a "hot spot".

In Barbados, Caribbean leaders hurriedly convened a meeting to discuss the "explosion", and to adopt a joint position towards it.

In Havana, Cuba, leaders of the Cuban Revolution dusted out maps to locate exactly where this little island was located.

The various reactions were indeed apt for a history-making event, which caught all by total surprise. Like a ball of fire, the first successful revolution ever to take place in the English-speaking Caribbean had burst on the scene.

It took four and a half years; an intense campaign of destabilisation by the United States and their Caribbean counterparts; outside interference in the internal affairs of the New Jewel Movement (NJM); mistakes by the young revolutionary leaders; and finally 20,000 American soldiers, supported by two aircraft carrier groups, to turn back the Grenada Revolution.

Even then, it still took six days of fighting before the US Goliath could silence the Caribbean David of scarce 350 square kilometres, and 100,000 people. Indeed, the then Chairman of the Joint Chiefs of Staff of the US military commented on the invasion by saying: "We got more resistance than we expected."

That invasion marked the very first time that the US had intervened militarily in the English-speaking Caribbean. It sparked off a mini-crisis between the American and British governments. British Prime Minister Margaret Thatcher personally and publicly condemned the invasion as an act of unprovoked aggression. Queen Elizabeth II, in her capacity as Head of the Commonwealth of which Grenada is a member, also publicly condemned the invasion.

In the United Nations, 109 countries supported a resolution condemning the invasion; only nine countries, eight of them participants in the invasion, opposed the resolution.

In many cities of Western Europe and Latin America, mass demonstrations protesting the illegal invasion, spontaneously broke out.

Following the invasion, the United States inspired the formation of the "Regional Security System" (RSS). It is an outfit combining the different Special Security Units (SSU's) of the then seven-island Organisation of Eastern Caribbean States (OECS), and the Barbados army. The RSS is trained and equipped by the United States and is regularly involved in joint military exercises in the Caribbean Sea with forces from the US and other NATO countries.

We Move Tonight

All this demonstrates that it is no hyperbole to state that the success of the Grenada Revolution on March 13th 1979, and its survival for four and a half years, irrevocably changed the political landscape of the English-speaking Caribbean.

And yet, the story of how the Grenada Revolution was made has not yet been told, in its entirety. This book aims to play a role in curing this defect.

The book contains three parts. Part A covers events from the latter half of 1977 to March 13th 1979. It is the story of **how** the Grenada Revolution was made. I had the privilege of being an eye witness and participant-observer in many of the historic events of that period. For those events I did not directly witness, I had the privilege of learning of them through countless discussions with persons who witnessed and/or participated in them.

Part B provides background to, and the context in which, the events described in Part A took place. Part B focuses on the period from November 1970; the period leading up to the formation of the New Jewel Movement in March 1973. However it goes back to 1951 when Eric Gairy, whose regime was overthrown in 1979, made his entry on the Grenadian political landscape.

Part B also, importantly, assesses the failure of the 1973-1974 Revolution, as that period of political turmoil in Grenada is regularly described. It also describes and examines the methods used by the NJM to regroup and build up, in tandem, the political and military machinery which would ultimately defeat the Gairy regime on March 13th 1979 and thereby unleash the historic Grenada Revolution.

Part C contains the author's retrospection from within prison on the tragic demise of the revolution, and his reflections on changes in Grenadian society which he observed on being released.

*

PART A

We Move, Tonight!

*

Chapter 1

NLA Recruit

It is September 1977. My friend Leon Cornwall invites me to accompany him on a visit to Hudson Austin at his home in the suburban community of Mardi Gras in St. George.

As we walked into his room, Austin was lying on his bed reading. Cornwall sat down. From his body language, it appeared to me that Austin was expecting us. With a gentle movement of the hand, he invited me to sit down. After about two minutes, Austin laid down his book and stared at me menacingly. Then he said, "Comrade Bogo, I think we have some business to deal with." With those words he arose from his bed.

With intense curiosity, I kept my eyes fixed on him, observing his every move. I was interested in knowing what that business was. Cornwall had simply told me, "Let's go by H.A. I have to check him on something."

Then Austin, dressed in short pants, his legs forming a conspicuous K, his hands behind his back and eyes focused on me, as if piercing through me, said in a dry, almost questioning manner, "Comrade Cornwall has a very high opinion of your

1

revolutionary commitment. He has recommended you for membership in the NLA."

"What is the NLA?" I asked.

"The NLA is the military wing of the New Jewel Movement which will deliver the Grenadian people from the clutches of Gairyism," Austin replied.

"Comrade, I'm ready to join," I said.

He smiled. Then he said in a slow admonishing tone, "Too fast, Mr. Layne!."

I could have kicked myself for my tactlessness.

In a grave and solemn voice, Austin then delivered a lecture on the National Liberation Army (NLA): its mission and seriousness; and the demands it made on its members. He said that members of the NLA could be called on at any moment to give their lives to the struggle. He emphasised this. All this time his eyes remained fixed on me. I was conscious that he was testing me, sizing me up. I consciously stared him back, straight in the eyes.

Then came the question, "Comrade Layne, are you prepared to join the NLA?"

"Yes, Comrade, I am prepared to give my life to the struggle." This time I believed I said it with sufficient but not too much eagerness.

"OK. You will be accepted as a member of the NLA," Austin rejoined. He then took out a document from his pocket, and laid it on a stool. "You will have to take this oath," he said, pointing at the paper. With deft movements he took a few steps, opened a cupboard, rose on his toes, beyond his normal five feet nine inches, and stretched his hand as if searching. He came out with a .38 Smith and Wesson revolver. He laid it on the piece of paper.

My father had been a senior police officer for many years, and thus I had seen and indeed handled many weapons, but I was impressed.

"Please get down on your right knee," Austin next said. "Place your right hand on the weapon," he continued. As I did this he read out the oath.

"As a member of the National Liberation Army, a fighter for the cause of the Grenadian working people, I pledge: that I will be ever faithful to the programme and policies of the New Jewel Movement; that I will diligently carry out all tasks assigned to me; and that I will not flinch from any danger, nor spare life itself in the struggle to liberate the homeland from the clutches of dictatorship."

"I pledge," I responded, and breathed a sigh of relief. But before I could raise my head, he said, "You are not yet through." He placed his hand in his pocket and came up with an oversize pin. He handed it to me. He pointed at the paper on the stool and said, "You must sign this with your blood, by way of your right thumb."

Goose bumps took control of my body. But there was no turning back. I realised that I had given my life over to the revolutionary cause; a cause which always filled my heart. I took the pin, pierced my thumb, and signed the oath. The pin-prick went to my heart. I was a member of the NLA! That was September 1977.

The National Liberation Army had been formed in 1973. Its emergence was a natural outgrowth of the formation and immediate popularity of the NJM and Gairy's ruthless response to this new political movement whose aim was to put the brakes on his banana-republic style of colonial dictatorship.

In the period 1973-74 the NJM launched its first major challenge to Gairy's power, in what some describe as the 1973-74 Revolution. In that period, which led up to independence, the NJM spearheaded an alliance of anti-Gairy forces in an effort to remove Gairy from power prior to independence date on 7th February 1974[1]. The effort failed. And so the 73-74 challenge was defeated[2].

That defeat took a heavy toll on the NJM, as many activists became disillusioned. The NLA also suffered as a result of the defeat. It experienced a decline and rapid turnover in its membership, as members left Grenada or simply dropped out. Additionally, the NLA lost a section of its membership, including some key activists, who disagreed with the party's political strategy. Some persons also parted ways with the NLA out of dissatisfaction with the positions they held within it. The NLA, like the NJM itself, therefore, faced the task of soul searching and rebuilding.

But by the time I was recruited the NJM had gone a long way in the process of rebuilding. The despair following the 1974 defeat had eased and hope and optimism of removing Gairy from power had been largely restored. The success of the party in regrouping was manifested in Grenada's first post-independence elections in December 1976 when the NJM-led People's Alliance came within 78 votes of winning based on the official figures. Yes those were the official figures. But the widespread perception locally and regionally was that Gairy had stolen the elections[3].

Notwithstanding the allegations of fraud and the disappointment that Gairy had survived yet another challenge, there were important political gains coming out of the elections. For one, Gairy no longer had total dominance of the parliament. He now had a 9-6 majority. Among the 6 opposition parliamentarians were the three top NJM leaders, Maurice Bishop, Bernard Coard and Unison Whiteman. And Maurice Bishop was named Leader of the Opposition. The writing was on the wall for Gairy.

My recruitment into the NLA was an example of the dialectical relationship that existed between the work of the party and the task of building the NLA, which is described in greater detail in Part B. I had been an active participant in the revolutionary struggle in Grenada since 1973. From then until 1977, I was very active in the students' movement. And though not a member, I was involved in the work of the Organisation for Revolutionary Education and Liberation (OREL)[4]. But it took the reorganisation of the party in 1977 to finally draw me into the structure of the NLA[5].

Indeed, it was only after I became a member of the NLA that I realised that I had been involved in its work since 1974, though on the periphery. I had carried out many small but important tasks on behalf of the NLA. My brother, older by four years, assigned these tasks to me. After joining the NLA, I found out that he had been a senior member of the NLA. Sometimes he would ask me to deliver some food or clothing at a particular location for him; or carry out surveillance of an area or building for some hours. I had always performed these tasks with great enthusiasm, feeling as though I was making the greatest and most important contribution to the struggle. And I displayed, I believe, obvious willingness to take on increasingly more daring tasks, at times proposing some of these myself. In short, I believe it was clear that my heart was crying out to play a more active role. All that time, I never knew that there was a separate military wing of the movement. I was to join it only later.

It was through my work as a member of the NJM Youth and Students Committee, together with my friend Cornwall, that I was recruited into the NLA. Cornwall was the chairman of the Youth Committee. After the Revolution, the Youth Committee ripened into the National Youth Organisation (NYO) and Cornwall became its first president. He also attained the rank of major in the People's Revolutionary Army (PRA) and was, up to the invasion, Grenada's ambassador to Cuba, Nicaragua and Mexico, among other countries.

Four months before I was recruited into the NLA, Cornwall systematically assessed my fitness for membership. The assessment process was an interesting one: never once was I told or did I suspect that I was being subjected to a "feeling out process" as it was called. Through our several joint tasks, he observed my seriousness, discipline and dedication. Through numerous discussions he ascertained my attitude to the armed struggle, and my ability to be confidential with sensitive information. It was only after he was satisfied with what he observed that he recommended me for membership in the NLA.

As a member of the NLA, I was called upon to keep security watch on the homes of Bishop, Coard and Whiteman. I was also involved in mounting security for meetings held by the NJM in different parts of Grenada.

I vividly recollect one such meeting in St. Patrick, the northernmost parish in Grenada. It is 26 miles from St. George. The meeting was scheduled for 7:00 p.m. Those of us responsible for security at the meeting arrived in the area at 6:00 p.m. Lester Redhead, a participant in the March 13th attack on the True Blue barracks, and later a captain in the PRA, was the person overall responsible for organising security in the area. He was then only 17 years old. He scouted the location of the meeting and the environs and noted vantage-points, observation points and escape routes. We were a security detail of ten persons. Redhead assigned a sector for each of us to observe. He also informed us of the communications signals to be used for the night. These signals consisted of words and signs.

Then about 7:00 p.m. Maurice Bishop, Bernard Coard, Unison Whiteman, Selwyn Strachan and other leaders of the NJM arrived. Over 1,500 people turned out to the meeting which lasted about two and a half hours. Although all the speakers received warm applause from the crowd, Bishop was the main attraction.

Indeed, he was always the main attraction at public or semi-public meetings. I remember him that night lighting up St. Patrick with his brilliant oratory. The sight of the masses rising to him as he denounced the corruption and abuse of power of the dictatorship is impossible to forget. With simple words, which the smallest child could understand, he gave a vivid depiction of the Grenada NJM wanted to build. A Grenada summed up by the main slogan of the party: "Let those who labour hold the reins." And he called on the people to struggle to turn the dream of a Jewel into a reality. The masses just loved him for such performances! His relationship with the younger generation was that of a committed and much admired brother while the older folk, especially in the rural areas, related to him as a favourite son who had 'raised their nose several inches'.

After Bishop completed his speech, the leadership milled around for about 30 to 45 minutes intermingling with the people. This was nearly always the pattern at these activities. Old folk would walk with cakes or sandwiches or homemade drinks and insist that the leaders share them. People would raise personal problems with the leaders and many jokes would be shared and laughed at. And most times after these meetings the leadership would stop off at the home of some prominent supporter in the area to have more drinks and enjoy village 'ole talk'. During all of this, the NLA members on duty would maintain unobtrusive vigilance. However, on that particular night in St. Patrick after the general intermingling with the masses, the leadership departed for St. George.

After their departure, Redhead called us together and we too departed. None of us bore weapons while we were on duty, but each of us knew what we had to do in case the need for weapons arose. Two days previously weapons were brought into the area. Two days after, they were removed. Security concerns had been raised: the party leadership had to be carefully protected, even at this very early stage as a top priority.

My main task as a member of the NLA was organising an NLA unit in St. David. In the 1973-1974 period, the NLA was well represented in that area. However, for diverse reasons, after the defeat the NLA lost most of its membership in the area. As a teacher at the St. David's Secondary School (SDSS), I lived in the parish during the week. Additionally, I was actively involved in the political work in the parish.

Indeed, I was a member of the Organizing Committee (OC) of the party, representing St. David. I therefore had ample opportunity to develop links in the area, and to pursue the task assigned to me by the NLA.

I was adequately equipped with necessary techniques to organise the unit. I received classes from Austin, Cornwall and Basil 'Aki' Gahagan in how to accomplish the task. The first stage in the process was that of identifying persons who it appeared to me were capable of becoming NLA members. Then through a process of observation and testing, in the manner Cornwall did with me, I was to select the best persons and organise the unit.

I was instructed that the members of the unit should only be told that a national command existed. They were not to be told who the members of the command were. They were to know of no one but me.

I threw myself wholeheartedly into the work, and identified a number of persons from different walks of life. There were workers, students, teachers, farmers, unemployed youths and self-employed persons. However, before I could approach anyone of those persons to become members of the NLA, a dramatic development took place.

Chapter 2

The 'Twelve Apostles'

Toward the end of November 1977, Gahagan contacted me. Gahagan was recognised as Austin's deputy in the NLA. He was second in command to Austin on the attack on the True Blue barracks on March 13th, and subsequently became the first Chief of General Staff of the PRA. Gahagan told me that I had been selected to travel overseas to receive military training. The NLA was clearly serious business! More serious than I had reckoned! True to the oath I took, I told him that I was ready to fulfil any instructions given to me by the party or NLA. I was told to report to a meeting at the home of Bernard Coard.

At the home of Coard I met Austin, Gahagan, Cornwall, Redhead, Einstein Louison and five other comrades. Coard was the last person to enter the living room where we were all gathered.

With an ease, which belied his 280 odd pounds, Coard took his seat. Immediately he began speaking. In his direct style he stated the purpose of the meeting: important matters of the NLA.

"The party has secured fraternal assistance for the NLA. A group of NLA members are to go overseas to receive military training. You have been selected as the 12 apostles," Coard said. He paused for effect. Then he stared at each of us in turn.

Twelve? I questioned myself. There were only 11 NLA members in the room.

"Remember, this meeting never took place," Coard next said, rising with a big grin on his face. "Later!" and he was gone.

Austin took over. He said that we had to be ready for departure in two weeks. Each of us who was employed had to obtain leave. We were not told our destination, nor given any other details. And no one asked any questions. However, as imagination runs, visions of Cuba began swimming before my eyes.

In the two weeks after that historic meeting which never existed, like the other apostles, my entire mind was focused on preparation for departure. For a cover story, I settled on attendance at a youth meeting in Barbados. Through our contacts we found out that a genuine youth conference was indeed taking place in Barbados. Thus if my cover was followed up, it had a good chance of withstanding scrutiny. Cornwall and Gahagan organised cover stories similar to mine. All three of us were secondary school teachers. We therefore needed only one week away from school in addition to the regular Christmas holidays.

One week before departure, we again gathered at the home of Bernard Coard. Coard asked each of us in turn about our cover story. In that session, Coard, ever the perfectionist, was at his vintage best. Like a professional interrogator, he questioned each of us in detail about our cover story. Many weaknesses were revealed in several stories.

For example, in the case of two persons, their story was that they were going on a fishing expedition; yet they were leaving the country via the airport. In another case, someone was going to Trinidad to trade agricultural commodities. Such trade is normally done via schooners – by sea; yet he was leaving via the airport. He had no plans to take even a box of bananas.

Each time such flaws were detected, Coard delivered a lecture on the need for attention to even the minutest detail. Sometimes, he came over rough; other times obsessive, even rude; and other times logical, didactic, and even condescending. But he got the point across: this was serious business!

One detail was added to my cover story. It was decided that arrangements would be made to post a Christmas card to my family from Barbados, explaining that I had to stay in Barbados longer than expected, since I had gained selection on a special committee which was meeting after the conference.

After the cover stories were settled, Coard addressed the matter of transportation arrangements for going to the airport. He lectured us on – if you believe! – the fact that for countless reasons transports do break down.

"It would be a disaster for any of you to arrive at the airport late," he warned. "Every one of you must organise for there to be a backup to the transport you are travelling in. In this way, if that transport breaks down, then the backup is available."

He was being fastidious I thought, but he was logical. And we all knew that when you could not defeat Coard's logic, to challenge him was to invite lectures. So after some more discussions, transport arrangements along the lines he insisted were settled.

Thus one week before departure, as Coard would have said, "All systems were in place and ready to go."

On the day before departure, I had my first contact with Maurice Bishop in my capacity as a member of the NLA, and in his capacity as chairman of the Security and Defence (S&D) Committee of the NJM. The S&D Committee was a special committee of the party headed by Bishop. It was exclusively responsible for the military affairs of the NJM. In this respect it was like the general staff of the NLA. Of course, Bishop and I had been together in many different settings before, but never in a military capacity.

We went to Bishop's home to obtain finance. Bishop, ever the charmer, placed us all at ease. Each of us present was given $120 (US) to cover expenses, and for contingency.

Bishop then told us, "The party and I personally are confident that you will equip yourselves to free Grenada from the rotten dictatorship....Just do your best".

He made each of us feel really special as he spoke. By the confidence he expressed, he inspired confidence in us. He possessed that rare and special ability and charisma to address a group of people and yet have each one feeling that he, personally and alone, was being addressed.

So less than one year after the NJM-led People's Alliance had come within a handful of votes of removing Gairy from office through the ballot box, the NJM was about to take a watershed step down the road of the military overthrow of Gairy. As a young revolutionary, I had no qualms about this move. The legendary Argentinean born Cuban revolutionary, Che Guvera, was my idol. His clarion call was to arise against oppressors by launching arm revolution throughout the third world. In my young mind, Gairyism represented one of the most rotten forms of dictatorship; and was I ready to answer the call of Comandante Che.

But, indeed, Gairy had sowed the seeds for that move by the NJM. The violence he unleashed on the young revolutionary movement in the early 1970's, culminating with the brutalization of the NJM Six on 18th November 1973[6], was still a fresh wound in the minds of Grenadians. The widespread perception that Gairy had stolen the 1976 elections had led to the view that he would never give up power by peaceful means. And then came 3rd January 1977[7] closely followed by 19th June 1977[8]. And so, while seeking to repress,

Gairy inflamed passions and cultivated revolution. Newton's law of opposites and the law of unintended consequences were at work.

On a Sunday in December 1977, twelve Grenadians left the country. There seemed nothing unusual about that. After all, many people were leaving. Some were going out of Grenada to do business and to return in time for the holidays. That Sunday was an historic day for the NLA. If ever there were any doubts in our minds that we would liberate Grenada, they all dissipated that Sunday.

The 12 apostles left Grenada at different times of the day, in small groups. Initially each group headed for a different destination. But we expected to regroup at our final destination within 24 hours.

My friend Cornwall was the advance man for one route. His task was to arrange flight connections from the stopover country to the final destination. Having made arrangements, he waited at the airport of the stopover country. He was awaiting Austin and a small group. He related his experience to me.

"Ache," he said, "when the plane on which I expected the General landed, I rushed to the balcony. I took up a vantage point so that I could see him as he emerged from the plane and he could see me. This was to avoid any mix-up. People began disembarking from the plane. After a while I became a little bit nervous because I did not see the "G". It crossed my mind in those moments that maybe something went wrong. My heart was beating heavily. Soon the line of people emerging from the plane got thinner. But still no General. My heart was really pounding now. And then, like a figure out of Wall Street, the General, well dressed and carrying a briefcase, emerged. Ache, you should have seen him. The man came off the plane as if he was in charge of the country!"

The military training course was of four weeks' duration. Throughout, we maintained a high level of discipline. We had strict instructions to refrain from loose talk. We were not to reveal our real identities to anyone. Not even to our instructors. Each of us used a nom de guerre. Austin was referred to as Cambridge, Cornwall as Elysee, Redhead as Glenroy, and I was called Street. We received instructions in guerrilla warfare tactics, reconnaissance, explosives, weapons, firing, field-craft, constructing booby traps, and physical training.

The course was very intensive and demanding, but it passed without any great incident. Cornwall sustained the only injury. He lost three teeth when the blank firing attachment from a rifle accidentally came off during an exercise and hit him in the mouth.

All 12 'apostles', including the last of the 'apostles', the only woman in our ranks, achieved excellent results.

But whenever I think about those memorable days, my mind goes out to Austin. I have some vivid recollections of his performance on that course. At that time he was 40 years old, by far the oldest of us. Indeed, he was of an age to be the father of many of us. Additionally, he had an injured knee, which pained him regularly. But those disadvantages in no way affected his enthusiasm and total participation in every aspect of the course. And his presence and enthusiasm were an inspiration to all of us.

On one particular morning, we went on a ten-kilometre run. The route was through thick jungle. We never used public roads or trucks, for fear of exposing our presence. This was an important condition throughout the course. Austin on that day gave what I considered to be an incredible performance. With a knee band on his right leg, and in obvious pain for the entire ten kilometres, through rough terrain, and by dint of sheer determination, he kept up with the group. More than once I decided to drop out under the pressure of the intense pace. But just seeing Austin and remembering that he was 20 years my senior and with an injury to boot, I was deeply motivated to continue. At the end of the run, I was heartened to find out that I was not the only person inspired by Austin's example to complete the course.

At the end of the course, we departed as we came: at different times and via different Caribbean islands. We returned to our homeland more prepared, and more confident of victory than ever before.

On my return home, my father asked me about the conference. I expected that. I gave him a 15 minute summary of the 'conference'! I had really practised that. I had to be careful to give him mostly generalities, with just enough details, which I could easily recall, to satisfy his detective mind. To this day I'm not certain if he suspected anything. We have never discussed it. But I would swear on the graves of my ancestors that the detective was fully 'bought'! In fact he implicitly praised my solicitude in informing the family of my delayed return, by sending them a beautiful Christmas card. Even as my heart weighed down with grief at having to deceive my father, I could not help but smile as I accepted his praise.

Chapter 3

Building the NLA

Shortly after our return to Grenada, we received a scare. On January 4th 1978, a minister of the Gairy government was assassinated. He was Innocent Belmar. Belmar had become notorious as Gairy's most brutal policeman. He was forced to resign from the Royal Grenada Police Force after the Duffus Commission of Inquiry, which investigated the brutalities that took place in Grenada in 1973-1974, stated in its report that Belmar was not fit to hold any position in the force.[9] With typical contempt, Gairy selected Belmar as a candidate for his party in the 1976 elections. Belmar ran in one of Gairy's strongholds and won a seat in Parliament. He was thereafter appointed a minister in Gairy's Cabinet.

The police accused Kennedy Budhlall of assassinating Belmar. They issued a "wanted" notice for him, which was announced regularly over Radio Grenada. Budhlall at the time was publicly identified with the party. This was so even though he and his group, based in Tivoli, St. Andrew, had effectively withdrawn themselves from the party's structure. As such, at best they had an alliance relationship with the NJM.

The party leadership apparently formed the view that the Tivoli group had carried out the act. This view was based

16

primarily on the fact that members of the group had in the past strongly advocated such acts as part of the means to remove Gairy from power. The leadership was strongly opposed to such tactics. This difference was one of the main factors responsible for the Tivoli group breaking away from the party.

I remember Cornwall, Gahagan and I going to a house in South East St. George some days after Belmar's death. There we met Bishop, Coard and Whiteman. They were in hiding. This was a precautionary measure against any retaliatory action Gairy may have had in mind.

Whiteman was lying on a bed, Coard was seated on the same bed and Bishop sat on a stool, smoking. Coard did most of the talking. He was almost uncontrollably angry. He described the assassination of Belmar as an act of madness. He said that it had the potential to throw back the struggle; that Gairy could use it as an excuse to declare a reign of fascist terror on the country; that this could greatly reduce the political space available to the party to build up its organisational work among the masses; and that it could seriously hamper the work of building up the NLA, since Gairy, in the wake of the assassination of his number one gunman, would raise his guard. Coard compared the assassination of Belmar to the wounding of a lion.

"The wound only makes the lion frantic, more desperate and ultimately more dangerous," he said. "If you want to kill a lion, stab it in the heart. This simple truth," Coard cursed, "has never been appreciated by the Tivoli comrades."

Bishop, chain-smoking throughout, supported Coard's view. Whiteman in his soft-spoken way also supported Coard's view.

However, Bishop, Coard and Whiteman said that we could not let the incident paralyse the movement. They set us the task of organising security for them. We were also instructed to mount a watch on Gairy's home, and on police headquarters, with the objective of discerning Gairy's intentions.

And then I experienced the great humanity, empathy and perspicacity of the NJM leaders. During the tirade against the Tivoli group I said to myself, "Boy, these men will order the immediate hanging of the whole Tivoli group given half a chance...", so furious were they. But then again, I must admit that their anger at what they perceived to be an act of madness showed great maturity. For their position was at variance with that of broad sections of the masses, particularly the youth masses. The position of the masses was, "So what if Budhlall shot Belmar? Belmar has gotten nothing more than he deserved!"

The leadership's maturity despite the evident anger was crystallized when Coard said, "After all is said and done, incorrect as the act is, the broader circumstances and the motivation involved cannot be ignored. The party, therefore, has a duty to assist KB" (Kennedy Budhlall). Bishop confirmed that the three senior leaders of the party were of one mind on this question. But ever the lawyer he shifted to examining the matter from a legal standpoint. He reminded Coard that Budhlall had not even been charged as yet. He said, "Look at the evidence on which we are accusing him: the members of his group have in the past advocated such actions; and the police have publicly accused him. Nothing else. I think that he is entitled to the presumption of innocence. It is not our job to judge him, but as a lawyer it would be my job to defend him." It was clear why he was considered to be the best defence lawyer in the country.

In the ensuing days, we fulfilled all the tasks assigned to us. Gradually the potential crisis passed. And, as promised, the NJM mounted a major local, regional and international campaign in defence of Budhlall and his co-defendant, Lauristan Wilson.

In court, Bishop led a powerful team of defence counsel from Grenada and the Caribbean. The evidence presented was highly contradictory and inconsistent. And the jury in the trial returned verdicts of not guilty in favour of the two accused.

Indeed, even before the matter went to trial, a strong public view was formed that the 'St. Andrew's Two', as they were called, were innocent; and that Gairy himself had organised to get rid of Belmar as a result of a rift between them.

After overcoming the small crisis and scare connected with the assassination of Innocent Belmar, the work of building the NLA continued full speed ahead. In the period January to November 1978, the main directions of that work were recruitment and training. This work was carried out islandwide. We ran training courses in St. George, St. Patrick, St. Andrew, St. John and St. David. Those members of the NLA who had received special preparation overseas carried out the training. Three incidents all linked to training exercises are imprinted on my mind.

The first of these incidents took place in St. Patrick.

Gahagan, Cornwall and I were training a group from the area. Dave Bartholomew, subsequently a member of the NJM Central Committee and one of my prison colleagues, led that group. We were camouflaged. We were demonstrating the field-craft technique referred to as the leopard crawl. While the class was in progress a farmer and two young boys, clearly his sons, suddenly and unexpectedly appeared on the scene. We all froze. This was hot stuff. The farmer came along. Tension as thick as fog hung in the air. We waited for an eternity, it seemed. The farmer walked straight on. He almost stepped on one of the participants in the class. We held our breath; then all heaved a sigh of relief as the farmer and his two sons walked by, and away not noticing a thing. When he was out of sight, we strengthened the observation arrangements and continued the class. The participants realised from that one experience that what we were saying to them only minutes before, about the effects of camouflage, was not merely theory. I still speak of this incident with a sense of genuine nostalgia and wonder.

The second incident occurred in the mountain area in the direction of St. John. Julien Fedon had used the area as a base during the 1795–1796 rebellion against the British. A group of 15 NLA members disguised as hunters went on a training exercise. We had a few shotguns and pistols.

Gahagan was the leader of the group. Cornwall, Einstein Louison, Chris Stroude and Conrad Mayers were also there. Louison was one of the apostles. He participated in the March 13th attack. He was a major and chief of staff of the PRA. Stroude was also a participant in the March 13th attack, a major in the PRA and one of my prison colleagues. Mayers, in late 1978 went off to join the US army where he attained the rank of sergeant. He returned to Grenada in 1982 to become one of the most outstanding field commanders in the PRA. He died tragically during the October 1983 crisis.[10]

We left very early in the morning for the mountain. We made our way through rugged terrain. Far up in the mountain, Gahagan selected an area to carry out the main exercise.

While the exercise was in progress, we heard a noise. Then suddenly, unexpectedly and unbelievably, we saw a farmer and cow appear. By then each of us was clad in military looking gear, lying on the ground, fully camouflaged and some of us had weapons in hands. We just froze. A pin drop could be heard. To tell the truth, I believe that every one of us was scared to one extent or the other. We could not have passed off our activities for anything else but military training. We had acted irresponsibly in not properly scouting out the area and organising better observation. If Gairy had obtained hard evidence of military training by NJM forces, that would have been equivalent to winning the lotto for him. The repercussions would have been devastating. The anger of the party leadership who had placed such confidence in us would have been ballistic.

We laid where we were while the farmer and his cow came on. There was nothing we could do. Our fate was in the hands of the gods. And the gods smiled on us. Miraculously the farmer and his cow passed between two comrades, within hair's breadth of each. Neither the farmer nor his cow observed anything. We got away by the skin of our teeth.

After that we went further up in the mountains, carried out the proper procedures, and accomplished a successful day's training.

On our way down we had another incident. Conrad Mayers fell and damaged a foot. As a result he could not walk. Tired and hungry, and traversing rugged terrain, we took turns in carrying Mayers.

The third incident is linked to the sea. We had a night-training exercise on one of the off-shore islands. A fishing boat transported us there. There were about 12 of us in all. The boat carried four at a time. On the final return trip, the engine broke down. Gahagan, Cornwall and I were in the boat with the operator. There was one other person whom I cannot recall. Although I could swim a bit, I hated the sea. I did not relish having to get out of that boat to try swimming to shore. Or worse still the boat going adrift. My heart was in my hands. Gahagan and the person I cannot recall were experts in the sea. And of course the operator was obviously an expert. And Cornwall could have handled himself. He had no dislike for the sea as I had. Although the others were concerned about the situation, they enjoyed themselves at my expense.

"Boy, the tide in this area really pulling," Gahagan said. "And the sharks? It is said that this area has the most sharks in all the sea around the island," he continued with an apparently grave voice.

"Two fishermen ran adrift from this area and they found them in Venezuela," the operator volunteered. "Their engine broke down; and the tide was so strong it took them away," he stated further.

Well, while the others were enjoying themselves, I was far from liking the situation. I wanted to ask the operator if his story was true; or if he was joking. But I was afraid of the answer. The last thing I wanted was confirmation.

Finally I said, "Is really a true saying you know, 'What is joke for school children is death for crapaud,'"[11] .

Eventually, by the skill of the operator we were once more set on the proper course. Gradually we made it to shore. As we approached the land, I was so relieved that without thinking I jumped off the boat. Splash! I landed in the water. I got soaked from head to foot. That produced the biggest laugh of all. It also proved the truth of the saying: "What is joke for school children is death for crapaud!"

We soon realised that my predicament had security implications. A nightclub was located almost exactly in the area we pulled up. People could have observed us as soon as we left the small beach area. It would have been unwise for me to be seen in the area wet from head to foot. That was bound to arouse suspicion. Moreover, as we soon discovered, the transport that was supposed to collect us was not on site. The driver of the car was Liam 'Owusu' James. During the Revolution, James was a member of the NJM CC and Chief of National Security. Later he would be one of my prison colleagues. But that night he was just a concerned driver. After waiting for hours to collect us, he became very concerned, bordering on frightened, and he left to obtain help to come in search of us.

With no car on hand as we reached the shore, I had to perform an operation to get from the beach area undetected. I went to hide in a nearby house, while Gahagan went off to arrange transport to take us from the area.

That night taught me another lesson: Never let the emotion of joy take control until you're out of the woods! Or the water, in this case!

And in this way, gradually, we built up the NLA island-wide. Austin, working directly in the St. Paul's area, and ably assisted by Redhead in particular and other apostles, had the greatest success. The St. Paul's area was part of the constituency which Bishop represented in parliament. It was a noted anti-Gairy community. The NJM was especially strong there. That strength showed up in the good results the NLA obtained in the area. But there is no doubt that much of the success achieved in building the NLA in that area was due to the inspiration which Austin imbued in the young NLA members.

Austin, as the recognised Commander of the NLA, also exerted great influence on the work of building up the NLA island-wide. He was an engineer by training. He specialized in road construction. He was also a building contractor. But his main strength was the ability to inspire young NLA members, to instil confidence in them. He achieved this mainly through the force of example, and by the confidence he always exuded. He not only taught a number of us how to make Molotov cocktails; he also participated in producing and stockpiling them. He did not just speak of the need for physical fitness; he showed us an example by keeping fit. He never demanded respect by asking for it; yet he expected it, and he extended respect to younger comrades in return. He was not a man for details, the kind of man to sit down and devise strategy and tactics and draw up plans – except for building houses! He stated openly and frankly that he left those matters up to the younger comrades. He particularly depended on Gahagan in this regard. And he always displayed utmost respect for our ideas, even though a number of us were young enough to have been his sons. In these small and unobtrusive ways he inspired in the young NLA members a profound commitment to the cause of the Grenadian working people; and confidence in and devotion to the policies of the party and its leadership.

Additionally, Austin's humour and affability allowed younger NLA members to be at ease in his presence. Many young NLA members, therefore, used moments with him to seek advice on matters related to the struggle and personal matters too. He was always willing to offer such advice. On the whole, as leader on the ground, 'Comrade H.A.' played a tremendous role in building up the NLA.

Chapter 4

"Barrels of Grease"

While the work of building up the membership and the military preparation of the NLA progressed, the S&D Committee tackled a separate but decisively important task: obtaining weapons to equip the NLA.

The police either recovered most of the World War II .303 rifles seized from Gairy's forces in the 1973–1974 period, or the NLA had lost control of them. Therefore, the NLA did not have any serious supply of weapons to depend on. Yes, there was the odd shotgun here and pistol or revolver there. But there was nothing else.

During the first half of 1978, the NLA mounted an operation to bring weapons into Grenada. A left wing movement in the Caribbean region promised those weapons to us.

The movement undertook to transport the weapons to the Caribbean Sea by way of vessel. Then utilising a fishing boat the NLA had to link up with the vessel, collect the weapons and deliver them on the East Coast of Grenada.

We Move Tonight

A number of NLA members, including myself, were mobilised to participate in the operation. At the time, the only compartment of the operation I knew of was that in which I was involved. On a number of nights Austin and Gahagan instructed me to proceed to a beach area on the East Coast. At least two other persons always accompanied me on those trips. We were told to keep watch. Each shift of three persons kept watch for three hours. We were looking out for a fishing boat. If we saw any fishing boat approaching the area, our instructions were then to send out a signal. The signal consisted of two long and one short flash of a powerful flashlight. If the approaching boat returned the signal, our instructions were to approach the boat cautiously, and from cover shout out the password "mango". We were simply told that if all went as planned then voices we knew well would respond.

After about a week of the operation, we were informed that it had been aborted.

It was after the Revolution that I learned the other details. Lester Redhead, Einstein Louison and a fisherman left Grenada to link up with the vessel. For navigation, they had an antiquated compass, maybe older than the three occupants put together.

Redhead related the story to me in prison. He said, "Three days come and go. But as the G-man [Austin] like to say, 'there was neither sound nor sight to serve us as a guide' to the vessel. We realised that we all lose. The captain didn't know head nor tail 'bout where we were. Man had to forget mission now and look for land. We were like Columbus. All we wanted was to see land so that we could make it to the nearest port. We dump communication equipment and all other things that could sell us.

"On the fifth day, we sighted land. We approached the land and pull up. Was only a few minutes we needed to know where we were. We couldn't miss the accent. We were in

Barbados. We told the people that we were fishermen, and that we lose. They gave us food and clothing in Barbados and navigation assistance to return home. Man was really disappointed that the mission fail. But was experience still."

Despite that failure, the party leadership, through the S&D Committee, did not give up the effort to equip the NLA. After other frustrations, we won the lotto in August 1978.

Cornwall and I were seated on the steps of a downtown St. George business place. We were weary! For over 30 hours we had gone without sleep. We were 'on our ears' as the saying went. We were struggling to put out an edition of *Fight*, the party's newspaper directed at youths and students. *Fight* was a fortnightly newspaper. However, an edition had not been put out for many weeks. The Organising Committee (OC) of the party which was chaired by Coard and was responsible for supervising implementation of all the organizational work of the party, had finally taken up the matter, and lit a fire under us to get *Fight* rolling.

As we sat, fighting to overcome sleep, we saw Bishop, Coard and Vincent Noel[12] approaching. My heart skipped a beat as I saw them. So stinging was the criticism from the leadership over our failure to maintain the scheduled production of *Fight* that we were very apprehensive of seeing them. Both Cornwall and I had expressed the hope that the next time we saw Coard, Bishop and Strachan in particular, we would mischievously hand each of them a copy of *Fight* and demand payment.

Bishop spoke first. He said, "Drop everything you are doing and follow us." It sounded as a hold up. Seeing the bewilderment on our faces he said, "You will not be disappointed."

"Can we get something to eat first?" Cornwall asked. By that time it was past 2:00 p.m. and we had not eaten anything since morning.

"No need," Coard replied. "You will get much more than food."

And Bishop, Coard and Noel laughed out together. Their elation was manifest. Something had clearly happened. But they were not telling us. They were enjoying our discomfiture.

We followed them by car, and drove to the home of Bernard Coard. There we went to a small room downstairs. In that room there were four containers. Each container was boldly labelled 'GREASE'.

"Now gentlemen, you have work to do; the party's double-indemnity policy is contained in these," Coard said, touching each container in turn. By that we understood that the party leadership had secured a supply of weapons for the NLA: A double-indemnity policy! We were now capable of defending ourselves, and defeating Gairy.

For the next ten hours Cornwall and I, assisted by Bishop, Coard and Noel for a while, unloaded and cleaned 16 M-1 rifles, and over 1000 rounds of ammunition. All tiredness and thoughts of food disappeared. I think it would be correct to say that that one experience established bonds of friendship between Cornwall and me as never before. As we worked, we joked, we laughed, and we allowed our minds to go back to the past and forward to the future.

Cornwall was especially happy. At one time he told me that only a few days before, his wife-to-be in four months received confirmation that she was in circumstances. Then he raised his head and said, "Ache, the sperm of life is a joy to the heart." He raised a rifle and held it to his breast and said, "My dear wife carries the future generation, and these will help to make the revolution." No wonder he was a noted poet.

When we were through with the cleaning of the weapons, we loaded them into two cars. This completed our component of the work.

During the Revolution I learned about the other compartments. The same night that we loaded the weapons into the cars, half was transported and hidden in the east coast parish of St. David; while the other half was hidden in the west coast parish of St. John. In that way, all the eggs were not in one basket. The leadership had spent the better part of eight months deciding on secure locations to hide the weapons. They took into consideration the fact that Gairy's forces had already begun the practice of digging up floors, kitchens, farmlands, and breaking down walls in search of weapons. They projected the use of metal detectors in the same endeavours. And of course the party leadership bore in mind the necessity of quick retrieval at a moment's notice.

Bishop drove the car which took the weapons to St. David. Whiteman travelled in a backup car. The presence of a backup car meant that if for any reason the car carrying the weapons broke down, then a substitute was immediately available. Coard drove the other car with weapons to St. John. Strachan travelled in the backup car.

Within days, another group of NLA members removed the barrels with grease from downstairs Coard's home, and disposed of them in the Bacolet Beach area, in St. David. They were never told what the other original contents of the barrels were, or why they were disposing of them. They did not 'need to know' this to fulfil their mission.

Chapter 5

November 1978 Challenge and the Call to Arms

November 1978 marked another turning point in the history of the Grenadian people: in that month, Gairy by his actions made it clear that he was preparing to crush the NJM. He demonstrated that he was not prepared to allow any serious political challenge to his dictatorship.

The NJM had planned a massive rally for November 18th 1978. That day was the fifth anniversary of the vicious brutalization of the NJM six – Maurice Bishop, Unison Whiteman, Selwyn Strachan, Hudson Austin, Kenrick Radix and Simon Daniel. The situation at the time was in many respects reminiscent of November 1973. The people were ready to turn out in their massive numbers in a show of protest against the deteriorating economic and social conditions in Grenada. Far from improving after the 1973-1974 uprising, the living standards of the people had deteriorated further. By November 1978, unemployment was an astronomical 49% of the work force. Skyrocketing inflation wrought by the oil crisis which had hit the major capitalist economies – Grenada's main trading partners – in the first half of the decade; criminal profiteering by the business class, especially those sections aligned to Gairy; and the lower prices of Grenada's agricultural produce on the world market, resulted in lower real incomes and worsening standards of living for the mass of Grenadian households. The education and health systems, and network of roads in the country had become progressively worse, reaching by November 1978 a level of dilapidation far worse than in the pre-1973 period. Sexual harassment, long a problem under Gairy, assumed vulgar proportions. As unemployment increased, and jobs became scarce, Gairy himself, his ministers, and his allies in the bureaucracy and business sectors, used their control over scarce employment opportunities as leverage, to force increasing numbers of Grenadian women folk to prostitute themselves to obtain jobs or gain promotion – or simply to hold on to their existing jobs! While overt acts did not occur with the regularity of the pre-1973 period, the aura of police brutality continued to loom over all those who protested, or thought of protest. And victimisation remained just as intense.

At the same time, Gairy proved totally incapable of addressing the serious problems facing the people and thereby alleviating their hardships. He had no serious programme to remedy the situation. One lame attempt was made under a programme he named 'Operation Bootstring', which burst before it could get off the ground. Gairy's idea was to invite foreign investors to Grenada to set up screwdriver-type factories with a view to easing the unemployment situation. But his efforts met with total failure. Investors were not satisfied with the investment climate in Grenada. The simmering unrest in the country, very evident among the working class; the dilapidated state of the country's infrastructure; and the extraordinarily large cuts and payoffs Gairy demanded, turned away potential investors.

While hardship mounted, and while Gairy did nothing to seriously tackle it, widespread corruption by him and his cohorts continued with the dictator himself growing to a millionaire many times over, owning by March 1979, $25 million (EC) worth of property in Grenada alone.

From November 1st, 1978, scores of outdoor and indoor meetings were held by NJM throughout the length and breadth of Grenada. Thousands of people attended those meetings. A massive momentum was built up for the Bloody Sunday anniversary. The air of expectancy in the country was electric. Grenadians from all walks of life geared up for what was expected to be one of the biggest political activities in the history of Grenada.

And then a frightened Gairy struck. Ten days before the rally, Governor-General Sir Paul Scoon issued a proclamation banning all political activities and public gatherings for a period of two weeks. This was only the latest move by Gairy in the post 1973-1974 period to crush the NJM. All his previous attempts were frustrated. The NJM leadership had devised ingenious methods to overcome them all.

The first major move by Gairy in the post '73-'74 period to suppress the NJM came in 1975. Under the guise of a law to govern the functioning of newspapers, Gairy effectively banned the party's organ *Jewel.* The party leadership responded to this action by first challenging it; by defying it.

On the first day that the ban was to take effect, *Jewel* was printed as normal and was brought out on the streets for distribution. But Gairy was expecting the challenge. His forces were mobilised and ready. They moved in and seized all copies of *Jewel* that they could lay their hands on. In the process, they also meted out a severe beating on Kendrick Radix, resulting in him being hospitalised.

Thereafter, the party shifted tactics. The party leadership decided to continue producing *Jewel* illegally but clandestinely. For this task an underground network for production and distribution was developed and perfected over the years. By

1978 that underground machinery was well oiled and working full blast. In this way, *Jewel*, under the editorship of Selwyn Strachan for most of the period, came out religiously once per week. It reached inside 5,000 households, or one in every four households in Grenada. This feat was accomplished in spite of the fact that imprisonment and beatings were the price of being found in possession of a copy.

Additionally, by 1978, the NJM propaganda machinery also rolled out five other newspapers, each on a fortnightly basis, under the same conditions as *Jewel* was produced. ***Fight*** was directed at the youth and students; ***Workers Voice***, at urban workers; ***Cutlass***, at rural workers; ***Fork***, at the farmers; and a newspaper for women. These newspapers carried news, and championed causes affecting the strata to which they were directed. The party's propaganda machinery also rolled out on a regular, sometimes daily basis, pamphlets dealing with burning issues affecting the masses.

In addition to being editor of *Jewel*, Selwyn Strachan was also the head of the Publications Committee. The Publications Committee was responsible for the functioning of this giant propaganda machine, which played a major role in rousing the Grenadian masses against Gairy. Not surprisingly, therefore, frantic and continuous efforts were made to crush it.

Ironically, by sending the party's propaganda apparatus underground, Gairy provided a major boon to the NLA. Because of the fact that the price of being found with a copy was beatings and imprisonment, the underground production and distribution of the various organs served as an important school for testing, on a weekly basis, the courage, seriousness, discipline, resourcefulness and level of security consciousness of all those involved in that work. It was therefore only natural for prospective NLA members to pass through that school.

The proof of the effectiveness of the giant underground apparatus is borne out by the fact that not once did Gairy give up the effort to discover and seize the machines with which the party produced its newspapers. Searches were mounted, surveillance was carried out, yet all were defeated; and week after week the apparatus rolled off its material, agitating and sensitising the people in every nook and cranny of Grenada, to the corruption and incompetence of Gairyism. This deeply frustrated Gairy.

In 1975, Gairy also passed the so-called Public Order Act. The aim of the law was clearly to control the regularity with which NJM could hold public meetings. It was also intended to suppress those meetings altogether whenever Gairy felt the need. At least this was his hope. The Act required the obtaining of police permission for the use of public address systems. Throughout the 1976 elections campaign and after, the law was used in an attempt to cripple the party's public activity. At times the police would grant permission to use public address systems for a period of one hour. This they did even when it was clear that the activities would last for periods over three hours. And they would be on site to enforce the one-hour time limit. Other times they would grant permission and then withdraw it. And still other times they refused permission outright.

Also, the police nearly always refused permission for the use of public address systems to advertise meetings. Advertisement by way of public address system had been up to that time the traditional way of advertising political and social activities.

The party leadership responded to this move by addressing crowds, sometimes thousands strong, by shouting at the top of their voices. For this they needed, and received, the co-operation of the masses in most villages and communities of Grenada.

As to the advertising of meetings hundreds, sometimes thousands, of small slips were printed. These slips contained all the information about the meetings. They were distributed door to door in the relevant communities. This provided yet another activity for the NJM political machinery and yet another forum for the party to meet the people. Whenever these meetings were to be advertised in a community, the party activists in the area, often spearheaded by a member of the Political Bureau, would fan out. That member would knock on the door of each household in the community. He would deliver slips and at the same time he would spend some time in the household conducting discussions with the occupants about their lives, problems they faced, things on their minds, and the programme, policies and activities of the party. In this way sometimes, one community would be covered over a period of a few days. Thus the party further deepened its links with the people.

It was under such trying circumstances, resulting from the effects of the Public Order Act, that much of the 1976 elections campaign was carried out. So successful, though, was that campaign that, despite massive rigging, the People's Alliance, of which NJM was the spearhead and mainstay, won six of 15 seats in Parliament. Perhaps more significant and more frightening for Gairy, the Alliance 'lost' the elections by just 278 votes. And that is despite 5000 NJM supporters being left off the rolls (voting lists), 2000 Gairy supporters being listed more than once to vote (one was listed a total of nine times spread over nine polling divisions in five different but bordering constituencies), and hundreds of dead people having voted in this election. In St. Patrick East seat for example, the Alliance 'lost' by 60 votes; yet 30 persons registered as dead by the Registrar of Births, Deaths and Marriages, were officially recorded as having voted in that election; their names were ticked off by the returning officer as having shown up and voted in that Constituency![13] Bishop, Coard and Whiteman, the three senior leaders of NJM, won three of the six Alliance seats. And the six Alliance members elected Bishop Leader of the Opposition. In this way NJM was now also a parliamentary force in Grenada. To many, though, this election "result" confirmed earlier analysis that elections in Grenada could never be free and fair under Gairy's dictatorship.

But the NJM was a new type of parliamentary force. NJM made it clear that it was not prepared to operate in the way that parties with seats in Parliament traditionally operated. In the past both the Grenada United Labour Party (GULP) – Gairy's party – and the Grenada National Party (GNP) operated as 'once every five years' parties. They were active around an election, and then the people never saw them again until five years later when they wanted to once again ask for their votes. NJM intended to operate in a revolutionary way, by taking Parliament to the people, by continuing the struggle from amongst the masses, while at the same time struggling in Parliament. This revolutionary method was summed up by the slogan: "From the People to Parliament and from Parliament to the People."

But Gairy intended to have none of this. Though he found it impossible to curtail the party's mass activity, he certainly intended to control its parliamentary activity. By November 1978 parliamentary meetings had become a rarity. And on some of the few occasions they were held, Gairy contemptuously refused to attend. By that time also, Whiteman could no longer take up his seat in Parliament because he was suspended from the (Lower House) Parliament, and forcibly ejected by police after an altercation with Gairy.

However, Gairy's efforts to curtail NJM's parliamentary role also proved a failure. The NJM parliamentarians continued and, indeed, stepped up their activities amongst the Grenadian masses, addressing them in their capacity as the people's parliamentary representatives. They also travelled outside Grenada, visiting countries, and attending conferences in their capacity as parliamentarians; and Bishop, who was immensely popular in Grenada, also gained popularity in the English-speaking Caribbean countries and in North America which he visited in his capacity as Leader of the Opposition.

So by November 1978, all Gairy's efforts to crush NJM came to naught. Indeed, the several challenges posed by Gairy served to strengthen the party's organisational capacity, since the party had to constantly devise new and creative methods to overcome them. The manifestation of this growing organisational capacity was dramatised by the fact that, just before November 18th 1978, NJM was leading and carrying out 21 different struggles simultaneously, on behalf of the Grenadian working people. The party was leading Barclays Bank workers in the struggle to gain recognition for the Bank and General Workers Union (BGWU), of which the overwhelming majority of them were members. The party was leading the workers of the Coca-Cola Factory in a similar struggle. And most significantly, NJM had begun to make inroads into Gairy's hard-core mass base – the 2,000 agricultural workers in Grenada.

On three estates in St. Andrew the workers had turned away from Gairy's union – Grenada Manual Mental and Intellectual Workers Union (GMMIWU) – of which Gairy was the founder and President-for-Life, and of which the workers had been members for 27 years at the time: some of them never having received a penny in benefits for their contributions to the union. They sought out and received the leadership of NJM in struggles to obtain better working conditions. These were only a few of the 21 struggles the party was waging. More remarkable though, was the fact that these struggles were carried out without disrupting the other tasks of the party.

Thus by November 1978 it was clear that the work of rebuilding the party had gelled. The efforts in overcoming Gairy's many challenges, the countless hours of day to day backbreaking organisational work, had set in train a powerful political machine.

This machine merged, in a dialectical relationship, with the growing desperation of the masses for change, as the socio-economic situation deteriorated with alarming rapidity. And yet the masses had seen all their efforts to obtain change by constitutional means frustrated by naked electoral fraud. This chemistry of a highly organised, active, and militant political machine rooted amongst the masses; the desperation of the vast majority of the population for change, in order to tackle and ease the hardships of daily life, the result of deteriorating socio-economic conditions; and the frustrations in obtaining this change through constitutional means, leading to a conviction that it could not be so achieved, had by November 1978, transformed Grenada into a time-bomb. The dictator himself realised that; he was aware that the situation could not just go on in that way forever. He had to move on it! And so he issued a challenge to NJM by banning the Bloody Sunday rally.

But the party did not bite. It saw Gairy's challenge for what it was: an excuse to provoke an incident. Out of prudence, the rally was called off. But the cancellation was not announced until the last moment. For ten days Gairy was left guessing, and planning too.

On November 18th Gairy's army – the Green Beast – and police showed up in force in St. Andrew. After the Revolution we learned that Gairy had hoped that NJM would have attempted to go ahead with the rally. In this hope he was again one step behind NJM. The party had learned its lesson from the last occasion it had attempted to defy a ban on a public meeting.

That occasion was June 19th 1977. At that time an OAS Ministers' meeting was in progress in Grenada; NJM had planned a mass meeting in the Market Square in St. George, the capital, to coincide with the OAS meeting. Police refused permission for the use of a public address system for the meeting. The leadership, however, decided to go ahead with the meeting, and in defiance of the police to use a public address system. It was felt that with the international spotlight on Grenada, Gairy would show restraint. That a miscalculation. No sooner had the meeting started than police and 'Green Beast' descended on the Market Square and began shooting and beating. People bolted left, right and centre for safety. Bishop and other leaders of the party escaped by the narrowest margin. Women supporters of the party surrounded Bishop and made off with him, as the police gave unsuccessful pursuit.

In the overall melee, which resulted from the action of the police and Green Beast, one man, Alister Strachan, a party activist and NLA member, and the cousin of Selwyn Strachan, met his death. He had jumped into the sea to escape a group of Green Beast soldiers who were pursuing him. While he was in the sea the Green Beast kept up incessant rifle fire on him. Two days later his body was fished out of the sea. Scores of other people sustained injuries from beatings, or while trying to escape the melee.

Gairy, we learned, had in November 1978, hoped for a replay of June 19th 1977. He had given instructions to the Green Beast, to shoot to kill the leaders of the NJM if they attempted to go ahead with the November 18th rally.

That November challenge urged upon NJM the irrefutable conclusion that Gairy was determined to eliminate the NJM leadership. No longer could the evidence of eight years be disregarded: the unleashing of the notorious Mongoose Gang, Grenada's Ton Ton Macoutes, on the population; the brutality and beatings visited on the leaders of the party; the brutalities throughout the period of the 1973-74 revolutionary upsurge; the murdering of the party's supporters with impunity; the rigging of the 1972 elections when Gairy awarded himself 13 of the 15 parliamentary seats; the outright robbery of the 1976 elections; the intense efforts to crush the legitimate activity of NJM under the guise of law and through the use of violence; the emasculation of parliament; the growing ties with fascist Chile[14] and South Korea; the effort to murder the party leadership on June 19th 1977; and now the setting of another trap. It was clear that Gairy was not only not prepared to give up political power through the ballot box, but more ominously he was ready to murder those who posed any serious political challenge to him. A famous Caribbean calypso at the height of the 1973-74 revolutionary upsurge, satirising the dictator, had him say, 'All those who try to scare me are lying in their grave'. It appear that Gairy was preparing to prove the prophetic ability of the songwriter.

NJM could not sit idly by and like lambs allow the dictator to wipe it out. The leadership had a duty to Grenada, to its membership and supporters, and to themselves to resist. And resist, NJM intended to. Out of the necessity of self-preservation, and the desire to deliver our beloved homeland from the jaws of dictatorship, all NLA members were called upon to "be prepared" in the immediate period to overthrow Gairy by force of arms.

Chapter 6

To Kill A Lion:
NJM's Military Doctrine

In June 1978, I attended an NLA military planning session. It was the first time that I had the privilege of attending such a session. But before then, I knew that such meetings were taking place from time to time. That session took place at the home of Bishop. Besides Bishop, Coard and Whiteman, Austin and Gahagan were present.

Austin made a presentation on what he called the latest information on Gairy's forces. He spoke mainly about the physical characteristics of the True Blue barracks – where the Green Beast were stationed – and the police headquarters. Gahagan gave a report on the state of the work of building the NLA-recruitment, training, morale and such related matters. The other persons present asked many questions. Coard especially solicited lots of details. For example, he asked Austin to show him on a diagram, which Austin had drawn on a blackboard, the precise location of every window in the True Blue barracks, and every possible escape route.

On the whole, while the atmosphere of the meeting was very serious, there seemed to be no sense of urgency. The discussions that took place were more akin to a think tank session than a decision-making session.

In the months immediately following, I attended a few other planning sessions. But to me, nothing seemed to change. Even after the arrival of weapons in August, the atmosphere of the meetings continued to be rather pedestrian. Indeed, if I were not deeply involved in the work of building the NLA and if I were not privy to the information that weapons had already been brought into the country, I would have definitely concluded that on the question of confronting the forces of Gairy, NJM was nothing but a talk show. It is not surprising that this viewpoint was widespread amongst youths.

However, after November 1978, the atmosphere was completely different. All aspects of the NLA's work were conducted at a feverish pace. The planning sessions of the NLA took on a sense of pertinacity and immediacy. We were informed that the leadership had mandated Coard to take full charge of every aspect of the strategic, tactical and logistical planning for the overthrow of Gairy. Coard was undoubtedly the leading strategist and organiser in the party; therefore that decision demonstrated that the party was putting its resources where its mouth was.

The military strategy of NJM was very simple. It can be summed up in one sentence: To kill a lion, stab it in the heart!

This strategy amounted to a firm repudiation of terrorism. Terrorism was one of the alternative strategies which had struggled for ascendancy within the relatively young revolutionary movement in Grenada. NJM's position held that isolated terrorist acts could not have brought down Gairy; they were mere pinpricks. The only effect of such pinpricks would have been to make the lion more vigilant, more desperate, and more dangerous. Terrorist acts would have provided the dictator with a perfect excuse and justification to crush the revolutionary movement. Moreover, such actions would have been ultimately rejected by the Grenadian masses, and would thereby have alienated important sections of the people. If only for these reasons, NJM, as a matter of policy, considered terrorism as incorrect and dangerous, and rejected it on those grounds.

But many people, both inside and outside the revolutionary movement, held the view that to bring down the dictatorship, it was only necessary to get rid of Gairy; a terrorist act could do the trick, they argued. NJM rejected this position. The party held the view that although Gairy was the linchpin of his dictatorship, his regime comprised more than just him.

I once heard Bernard Coard express this position saying, "Gairy is gone. His Mongoose Gang and secret police remain. His entire repressive and political apparatus remains intact. They are seething for revenge. They feel justified in taking any action to avenge their leader's death ... they crush the revolutionary movement!"

Guerrilla warfare was another strategy that was flirted with by some within the revolutionary movement. That too was rejected by NJM. NJM's position was that protracted war was not necessary to defeat Gairy. Such a strategy would have provided time for Gairy to build up his forces, maybe even invite foreign interference, the party argued. Additionally, the view was held that the size of Grenada – 133 square miles – militated against protracted guerrilla war. It was the party's observation that in all the countries where guerrilla warfare as a strategy succeeded, revolutionaries had lots of physical space available. This physical space, it was argued, facilitated the survival of the guerrilla forces in early hit and run stage of the war, when preservation was the main objective, until they were able to gather sufficient forces and resources to stand and face the enemy in defensive action, before transitioning to the stage of launching conventional offensive actions. The main examples referred to in those days were China, Vietnam, Cuba, Angola, and Mozambique.

It was also a great concern of the NJM leadership that the pursuit of a strategy of guerrilla warfare could have resulted in a bitter civil war, widespread loss of life and destruction, and also the physical elimination of the revolutionary movement.

By November 1978 these questions of military strategy had been resolved. But they were still much talked about. Reason: it took years of arguments, recriminations and splits, before scientific, rational, responsible and sensitive solutions could be applied.

As I understand it, the main protagonists of the strategy of terrorism[15] were members of the Tivoli group, led by the Budhlall brothers. From 1973 onwards they argued bitterly for their position. They viewed the leadership's anti-terrorism position as a manifestation of fear of the challenge posed by Gairy. And they openly stated this. They had opposed the party's participation in the 1976 elections, on the ground that parliamentary struggle was irrelevant to revolutionary struggle. And they dismissed the NJM leadership as armchair revolutionaries sitting in St. George and just "talking shit".

Additionally, they held the view that in the effort to achieve political ends, no means were immoral. Nothing was out of bounds. They advocated co-operation with the CIA, through linking up with a Grenadian born reputed CIA agent. They rationalised their position by asserting that they could use the CIA by obtaining weapons and money for the struggle out of the reputed agent..

This position greatly alarmed the party leadership. It led to some nasty scenes on some occasions. I was told that on one occasion, in a heated argument, Coard accused the Tivoli group of being nothing but political cowboys who were objectively plotting the smashing of the party.

In my assessment, though, those guys were honest and genuine revolutionaries though they were mixed up in their thinking, and, not unlike many of us, immature at the time.

The guerrilla warfare trend was much more short lived. Gahagan was one of the principal protagonists of this trend. But it was the natural outlook of the majority of NLA members, most of whom were under 25 years of age. Loyalty to the party, confidence in the leadership and the power of reason, won our heads firmly to the position that this was not the correct path. But the idea never really died in our hearts. I knew as a fact that as late as March 12th 1979, though no member of the NLA advocated that path, a number of us would have embarked on it without hesitation.

Chapter 7

The Overthrow Plan

The plan for the overthrow of the Gairy dictatorship, which was drawn up in November-December 1978, can be divided into three stages:

Stage One: the initial attack. This stage was to be carried out by the NLA. In this stage, three targets were to be taken. *Target One*: the dictator himself. He was to be taken prisoner. *Target Two*: The Green Beast. They were to be dispersed and their weapons seized; but as many officers as possible were to be taken prisoner. This target was to be taken simultaneously with Target One. *Target Three*: Radio Grenada. The only radio station on the island. It was to be taken after Target Two and by part of the force assigned to that target.

In *Stage Two*, a general uprising was to be declared. The entire party apparatus islandwide was to be mobilised through telephone, runners, and other means of communication. Their task as foreseen was that of giving direct leadership to the masses in smashing the remnants of

Gairyism. Via Radio Grenada, the plan foresaw the masses being informed of the initial successes of the NLA, and being called upon to rise up and complete the overthrow of the dictatorship. The main military objective of this stage was to be the seizure of all 36 police stations islandwide, and thus the effective disarming of Gairy's repressive apparatus.

Stage Three was to be the stage of consolidation. The objective in this stage was to be the rounding up of all Gairy's key political organisers and political thugs, and thereby prevent any possible regrouping of Gairy's shattered forces.

The main thinking behind the plan was that the wily dictator, with his mystical hold over his mass base, and his army were the mainstay, the heart, of his dictatorship. These two targets, therefore, had to be taken first, and simultaneously. It was assessed that if those two targets were successfully taken – Gairy a prisoner and his army destroyed – then a serious physical and psychological blow would have been struck against the dictatorial machine.

That was seen as the equivalent of a man in a fight being knocked unconscious, and losing his right arm at the same time. He was bound to go down and remain flatfooted for a few hours. The seizure of Radio Grenada would then be the equivalent of taking away the fighter's tongue; so that by the time he slowly regained his senses, and awoke to what was happening, he would not be able to call on his friends to help him.

At the same time these initial blows struck against Gairy would have acted as an impetus, propelling the masses into action. In their thousands they would overwhelm the wounded and unconscious giant. They would ensure that by the time he awoke, he would be down and out, pinned to the ground. It was therefore the activity of the masses in their thousands, the general uprising, which would transform the initial successes of the NLA into the routing of Gairyism.

We Move Tonight

The main problem encountered in elaborating the details to implement the plan was to determine exactly where, and precisely how, the dictator was to be captured. This was a fundamental question; the solution to it was decisive in determining the form the entire operation would take.

There were three alternative solutions open to us on this question.

Alternative One: Capture Gairy at his home. There were two main problems with this. For one thing, Gairy was a cunning character. He was known to vary at random his sleeping location. We were very concerned about a situation arising where we mounted an attack on Gairy's home, only to find that he was not there. This possibility we could have minimised though, by mounting a 24 hour watch on Mt. Royal, Gairy's official residence. However, Coard was not satisfied with such a solution. He was worried that there may have been unknown routes by which Gairy could have slipped out of Mt. Royal unobserved.

The second problem was more substantial. We lacked detailed up-to-date information on all the physical characteristics of Mt. Royal. Coard was just not satisfied with the information we possessed. He wanted to know the location of every room in Mt. Royal; which room Gairy slept in; and every window in that room. There were rumours that Mt. Royal contained underground cellars into which Gairy could disappear and hide out for days. Coard operated on the basis that those rumours were true. Indeed, after the Revolution, one such cellar was detected in Mt. Royal.

Alternative Two: Capture Gairy at his office, which was located at the Botanical Gardens. Here again the random nature of Gairy's movements was a problem. There was really only one occasion we could have felt relatively sure of catching him: that was on the meeting day of his Cabinet. However, in late 1978, Gairy shifted his Cabinet meetings to the True Blue barracks.

A bigger problem though was that this alternative implied beginning the Revolution in broad daylight. That was a serious disadvantage.

Even so, that alternative was given serious consideration. Gairy and his Cabinet meeting in the army barracks, created a situation in which all his eggs were in one basket. It was an alluring situation. With one action Gairy's apparatus could have been dealt a crippling blow. The complications involved in taking Target One (Gairy) and Target Two (True Blue barracks) simultaneously would have been eliminated. On the other hand, though, the presence of Gairy in True Blue would have naturally caused the army to be more alert and vigilant. So, in the final analysis, it was decided that the disadvantages inherent in that model outweighed the advantages, and hence it was rejected.

Alternative Three: Capture Gairy on a Saturday night – early hours of Sunday, at his nightclub, or on his way to or from there. A Saturday night visit to his personal nightclub was one of the very few routine activities the dictator carried out.

After many sessions, Alternative Three was agreed to be the most propitious model. The planning stage was on the home stretch. The only thing left to settle were details. Important details though. Details capable of making the difference between success and failure, victory and defeat, life and death.

It is a Saturday night in January 1979. My friend and comrade, Liam 'Owusu' James, comes to my home. We leave together. There are four other persons in the car with him. Officially we are headed for BBC Nightclub in the southern part of St. George. Five times along the way he stops. Each time one of the occupants of the car drops out. He takes up an advantageous position. He observes the traffic closely as it passes by. Three hours later James returns along the same route. Five other persons are in the car. Smoothly, the changing of the guard is accomplished.

This ritual was carried out for eight Saturday nights in January and February 1979. In this way we gathered detailed and precise information on Gairy's movements to and from his nightclub.

However, the watch on Evening Palace nightclub itself normally commenced about 3:00 p.m. on those Saturday evenings. NLA members under the guise of running, or playing sport in the nearby playing field, visited the Evening Palace area. There they spent many hours carrying out observation. The main objective was to observe if any, and if so, what extra security arrangements, other than what met the eyes, were taken. In this way we found out that a search was usually made in the area of the nightclub about 6:00 p.m.; but no extra security force was brought in.

At 9:00 p.m. two undercover NLA members visited the nightclub as guests. They remained there until the club was ready to close. For a period of eight weeks the party provided $100 to each, per week, for these visits. With that money the NLA undercover members were able to spend and live up to the big life, while at the same time carrying out their main task of detailed observation. In this way we gathered information on the physical characteristics of Evening Palace, and Gairy's movements inside it. We knew that he always spent a period downstairs, on the first level of the nightclub mixing with visitors. After that he retreated to an ornate Gold Room where his many ladies took turns visiting him.

With this information, things were in place to activate the plan for making the Revolution. Indeed, most of us were of the view that things were in place as early as February 11th 1979. But there were to be four false starts before the Revolution got off the mark.

Chapter 8

Postponements

The first major disappointment came on February 9th. On that evening, leading members of the NLA gathered at the home of Bernard Coard. Austin, Gahagan, Cornwall, Redhead, Einstein Louison, Chris Stroude and Strachan Phillip were all present. Bishop and Coard were also there. The atmosphere of the meeting was tense and expectant. The general view among us members of the NLA was that we were meeting for the last time before the Revolution.

Austin gave a general report on the state of the NLA. Then each of us in turn filled in specific details. Bishop and Coard listened attentively. Throughout, Bishop's face, like a chimney, was enveloped in smoke. He asked few questions, leaving most of the interrogation to Coard.

The details of the planned attack were also discussed. Six men were assigned to capture Gairy. Those men were to be disguised in police uniforms. The idea was for them to enter Evening Palace just about 3:00 a.m. In this way we expected to penetrate Gairy's security ring. Simultaneously, the main strike force would attack the True Blue barracks. We expected that the element of surprise and the firepower provide by the 16 M-1 rifles would secure victory over the Green Beast.

Animated discussion took place on the details of the plan. Bishop and Coard were dissatisfied with many important areas. They felt that the details of the plan for co-ordinating the actions to capture Gairy with the main attack on the True Blue barracks were not thoroughly worked out.

Coard in particular insisted on that. "All the pieces must be in place before we make a move. This is not an election, where defeat could be redressed in five years time. In this game we either win or we die. There will be no comeback." It was vintage Coard!

Those warnings brought on an air of disappointment to the meeting, so geared up and ready to go were we. To us the thought of defeat was nowhere near our minds! That was just not part of our calculation. I felt at the time, and I think that the other NLA members shared the same feeling, that Bishop and Coard were making a big thing over matters that were of no significance.

It was Coard who put forward the position to call off the attack. "Comrades," he said, "there are still many loose ends to tie up before we are fully ready to launch the attack. I don't think that we can have everything ready before tomorrow night. Therefore, the attack cannot be carried out."

His voice carried the ring of finality. Everyone remained quiet. No one seemed sure how to react. The let down and disappointment took almost physical characteristics on the NLA members, as blood appeared to drain from our faces..

Then Bishop spoke. "In view of the situation, and the points made by Bernard, I don't think we can move. I can well understand the disappointment," he said, his voice carrying his sincerity, "but we have a responsibility to ensure when we move, that success is guaranteed. In the circumstances, therefore, I'm sure you would agree that the correct thing to do is to call off the attack."

It was a clear appeal. An appeal made in such reasonable words and fine style that no one could dissent. And so the attack was called off.

We Move Tonight

I remember Gahagan, Cornwall and I together walking away from Coard's house. We saw a police jeep patrolling. We looked at it.

Gahagan said, "I should be driving one of these Sunday morning." He had still not fully digested the fact that the attack was off.

One week later there was another postponement. Bernard Coard invoked the necessity of radio communications as a reason for this one. He said that the units assigned to take Target One (Gairy) and Target Two (True Blue barracks) needed to have radio communication with each other. And that the leadership needed to have communication with both units. Since his logic was sound, and his presentation persuasive, and since no radios were immediately available, a postponement was won on that ground.

However, I can well remember that meeting for another reason: a clash between Coard and Strachan Phillip.

Bernard Coard expressed the view that each NLA member should carry a length of rope on the attack. The rope he said was necessary to tie up any prisoners taken.

On the mention of prisoners Phillip interjected in his high pitched voice, a mix of Grenadian, Jamaican and British accents. He had lived in a Jamaican community in England for many years. He said, "We have no right to take any fucking prisoners mannn. Prisoners will only slow us up. It's simple mann; we shoot all prisoners and we move on."

Coard got angry. He described Strachan Phillip's statement as 'madness'. He said that such action would cause the Revolution to lose support even before it began; that even hardcore supporters of the party would oppose such actions; that Grenada was a very small country making up one big family; that almost every Grenadian including the firmest supporters of the party has a cousin or nephew in Gairy's army; and that they would not approve of their being gunned down in the manner proposed by Phillip. In fact the irony of the situation was that the Commander of Gairy's army was a close cousin of Bernard Coard, and Strachan Phillip had a nephew in the same army.

Strachan Phillip, by now as angry as Coard, responded, "My God! Bernard Coard wants to make a Revolution with a rope in one hand and a Bible in the next!"

Subsequent to that meeting, I learned that on a previous occasion, Coard and Phillip had clashed over the same issue.

On the third postponement, the fertile mind of Bernard Coard came up with yet another reason for delay. This time he said that the NLA needed to rehearse all the actions before the attack could take place. He suggested that the NLA should build mock-ups of the three targets to be taken in Stage One; and that we should practice on these mock-ups. He said that it was only after that that we would know if we were ready to attack. This was undoubtedly a proposal to postpone the attack in the immediate period.

I remember saying to Coard on hearing this, "Bernard, I don't think that this is necessary. We have sufficient information and knowledge of the targets to implement the plan. After all, history is full of examples of men crossing oceans to fight on other continents. Five hundred thousand American soldiers went to Vietnam. Did they prepare a mock-up of Vietnam before going there?"

Coard responded to me, and to others who questioned his position, by asserting that a mock-up was necessary. He said that we could not go forward before the mock-ups were prepared, and practice carried out.

While disappointment was the response to the previous postponements, on this occasion the response was one of anger. Deep, deep anger! Real anger! We formed the view that the party leadership had gotten cold feet and was looking for an excuse to abandon the attack. We placed responsibility for this squarely on the shoulders of Bernard Coard. I for one loathed every ounce of Coard's 20 odd stones at that moment. As far as I was concerned out of cowardice he had betrayed the Grenadian working people by calling off the attack.

After the meeting most of the NLA members who were present at the meeting at Coard's home went to the home of Strachan Phillip some two kilometres away. We discussed the situation. We decided to go over the head of Coard and appeal directly to the party leader.

That night Bishop was attending a public meeting in St. Andrew. We decided that a four-man delegation should go off to St. Andrew and discuss the situation with Bishop. Gahagan, Redhead, another comrade and I were members of the delegation.

We outlined our position to Bishop, with emotion born of conviction that everything was in place to move; that there was absolutely no basis for any further delay; that the continuous postponements were having a very negative effect on the morale of the troops; and that Coard's position of calling off the attack was nothing but downright cowardice.

Bishop listened to our views cordially and attentively. At the end of our presentation of views he said, "I will discuss the matter with Bernard," and he immediately changed the subject.

Then as only Bishop could do, he disarmed us completely by turning on his charm. Leaning on his car we just stood there rapping, laughing and enjoying cold beers –tension and anger no more. We did not leave until the meeting was over. We stayed and took in another Bishop masterpiece of a speech.

During the following week I was invited to a meeting at the home of Coard. Bishop, Coard, Austin, Gahagan, Cornwall and Redhead were present. Kennedy Budhlall was also present.

Although the Budhlall brothers and the Tivoli group had previously broken with the party, after Kennedy Budhlall was freed on the charge of murdering Innocent Belmar, he re-established close links with the party. And by January 1979 a good working relationship existed between NJM and elements within the Tivoli group, especially Kennedy Budhlall.

Both Bishop and Coard spent a great deal of the meeting questioning Budhlall and discussing with him, in general terms, strategy and tactics for the planned attack. Budhlall said that he was confident that he could provide 15 armed men to participate in the attack. The idea was for Budhlall to move men down to St. George to link up with the NLA forces for the attack.

Coard in his staccato style fired question after question at Kennedy. He asked Budhlall to give him details on the level of military and psychological preparation of each of his 15 men; and demanded information on the capability of each weapon Budhlall possessed. Not satisfied, he wanted a description of the technical state and capacity of each vehicle Budhlall intended to use to move his men. He wanted to know how quickly Budhlall could mobilise those men.

At one time, under intense questioning, in exasperation Budhlall expressed the view that Coard was trying to make a fool of him, or he was questioning his veracity.

Coard responded to Budhlall's irritation by saying, "KB, we cannot fight with good intentions and fine words. I know how these things work; you know I will only believe you when I can touch each of your 15men."

To me that entire meeting was pathetic; it was a sham. One could not but feel that the meeting was a tactic to placate the anger of the NLA members; and to give the appearance that the question of moving on Gairy was still under serious consideration. To this end we were told at the end of the meeting that the S&D Committee would consider the question of attacking. We were told that we should get in touch with Austin on Friday to know the position.

We Move Tonight

On Friday 2nd March, I phoned Austin from my work place in St. David. He told me, "We cannot purchase the goods this weekend." The attack was off. For the fourth time. And for all time it seemed.

Chapter 9

March 10, 1979: Election Ruse

In February 1979 the FBI arrested Chester Humphrey and Jim Wardally in the USA. Humphrey and Wardally were two Grenadian youths closely associated with NJM. They had been based in the US for several years. Wardally had a stint in the US army. Humphrey was one of the outstanding young revolutionaries coming out of the Black Power movement. He was one of the early members of the NJM Bureau. He migrated to the US in 1975 with the objective of studying medicine but he remained deeply committed to the cause of the NJM and the struggle of the Grenadian people. Humphrey and Wardally were jointly charged for illegally exporting weapons concealed in barrels of grease to Grenada.

The news of the arrest of Humphrey and Wardally sent shockwaves through Grenada. Gairy and his forces went into a frenzy. Searches were mounted left, right and centre. Rumours abounded like wildfire. Some said that NJM possessed automatic rifles; others said we possessed grenade launchers. The party neither confirmed nor denied these rumours. Instead we adopted the public position that "Gairy must now know that if he hit us we go fight back!" For every

Grenadian it was wait and see: tension and expectancy gripped every inch of the Grenadian landscape.

In the second week of March, Gairy unveiled his first move in his game plan for the new situation. It was an election gambit. In a ploy to throw the party off the scent of his real plan, the cunning Gairy sent out a stream of election signals. With vigour NJM took up the elections challenge. All party members, including members of the NLA, were issued instructions to gear up for elections. The Revolution was aborted! Or so it seemed. But Gairy ensured that was not to be.

It is Saturday March 10th 1979. The leaders and activists of NJM from around Grenada are gathered in a building in St. George. The special meeting is five minutes into its business. There is one item on the agenda: "Strategy for the impending elections."

Suddenly, a hysterical female party member bursts into the meeting. All heads swing in her direction as she shouts, "Police coming!" Excitedly she informs the meeting that Gairy's forces are breaking into the homes of Bishop and Coard. Bishop, Coard, Whiteman and Austin are 'wanted'.

With that, pandemonium breaks out. Everybody scatters. Bishop, Coard and Whiteman bolt in the direction of South St. George. Everyone makes it for his or her hole.

Later that night we found out that the meeting scattered just in time to escape Gairy's dragnet. The police had gone to the homes of Bishop and Coard. They expected to find them there. They were minutes too late. They found Liam Owusu James and Vincent Noel instead. They were promptly arrested.

Meanwhile, another large force of police and soldiers had gathered at the fire station, less than one kilometre from the location of the party meeting. They were preparing to fan out with the aim of preventing any possible escape by the NJM leaders. But they were late off the mark, and the NJM leaders beat them to the post by a head. Gairy had declared his hand. The moment of truth had arrived; and it was Gairy who had chosen the moment. The ball was now in his half of the court.

That night I went to St. David to inform the NLA members in the area of the situation, and to ask them to stand by. The NJM supporters throughout St. David were of one view: Gairy was not sincere about elections. "There is only one way to deal with Gairy," they said. "Grease him!"

Other NLA leaders also 'touched the ground' in their respective communities. Their reports were the same: The people, and especially the youth, were in a combative mood.

Chapter 10

March 11, 1979:
Grenada in Labour

Next day at 9:00 a.m. a friend and comrade of mine since school days visited me at home. He told me that the party leadership wanted to get my assessment of the present political situation. He told me that I had one hour to prepare it. And he left.

In about 1000 words I outlined my assessment of the situation. The bottom line of my position was summed up by the words: "Grenada is in labour! The people are ready to deliver the Revolution!"

As promised, my friend returned and collected the written document. He told me that I should remain at home; that he would get back in touch with me.

Within one hour my friend was back. He said that I must leave with him. I dressed. Not knowing the mission, I selected clothing capable of standing up to tough conditions. We drove for about one and a half kilometres. Then we turned off the main road. We entered a house located about 300 metres away from Mt. Royal – the official residence of Gairy.

61

There seated in a room were Bishop, Coard and Whiteman. This was hot stuff! More than real life it seemed. They were clad in underwear only. Their bloodshot eyes betrayed a lack of sleep. They greeted me in turns. My friend left.

Coard was the first to speak. He said, "You have displayed a serious lack of security consciousness by writing this." Boops! My heart collapsed, as I stared at the paper in Coard's hand, my handwriting unmistakable. "If Gairy discovers this he would be left in no doubt as to the intention of the party."

I felt he was overstating the matter, but what could I say? I had clearly made an error, and I recognised it. But I felt that it was unfair for the leadership to summon me in that way to criticise me on that matter. And my patience was wearing thin after the disappointment of the previous weeks.

"In future you must be more elliptical than this," Coard continued, disregarding my obvious discomfort. "We are not so unintelligent for you to feel the need to read and spell, dot all i's and cross all t's for us." It was unbearable. Then without change of tone he said, "In any case we did not call you here for this," and he crushed the paper in his hand. "We have serious business to deal with."

With that, almost as if Coard had used the words "Your Witness", Bishop took over. I had hardly caught my breath.

"Dakes", he alone called me so, "are you not overstating the mood of the masses?" was Bishop's opening question.

"No, I don't think so," I replied. I went on to describe to him a number of conversations and experiences I had the previous night, and indeed the previous days. "Even before Saturday," I said, "I approached a number of youths offering the voter registration forms. The majority refused the forms. You know what they told me? 'Give us some of the grease and we go vote against Gairy with it.' " Bishop listened to me patiently, and at the end he seemed satisfied.

"How many men do you think we can mobilise to launch the attack?" he asked, skilfully changing the line of questioning.

"I cannot say exactly," I answered him. "H.A. and Aki would be in a better position to answer that. But," I said, "I can mobilise 15 men from my unit for the attack." I was being deliberately optimistic. "But Maurice," I said, "I'm certain that once we make the initial move, we will get more forces than we have weapons for." That was my way of begging him not to put too much emphasis on the quantity of men available for the initial assault.

"Do you think we can successfully attack Mt. Royal and capture Gairy in there?" Bishop continued the questioning.

"Once he is there I have no doubt we can grab him! We only need six men for that!" I answered, not displaying any doubt or hesitation. I knew that my total confidence was at variance with Coard's concerns, but I could not care one lick about that at that moment. And in any case I had already dismissed Coard as a joker when it came to military matters.

But Bishop laughed as I gave my answer. How cocky I must have sounded!

"Besides you, who are the other five?"

"Any of the apostles," I responded almost before the last word was out of his mouth. I was sure on that. I knew that it was more than possible to accomplish that mission. And boy, the daring involved in it had such magnetic attraction that there would have been no shortage of volunteers!

And in this way the questioning from Bishop went on. After some discussion among the three NJM leaders, Bishop said that I should leave, and that I should contact Austin, Gahagan and Cornwall. He said that I should discuss things with them along the same lines as they discussed with me, and then I should report back.

With great enthusiasm I covered the three kilometres to the area of St. Paul's. There I contacted my friend Cornwall.

We discussed the situation. We had exactly the same appreciation: The birth of the Revolution was at hand!

We hurriedly contacted Gahagan. Then together we visited Austin. Austin was hiding out in the South East St. George area.

As instructed, I discussed the situation with all three. And as expected the consensus was – We must move!

By about 2:00 p.m., I was again in the presence of Bishop, Coard and Whiteman. I reported to them. They listened attentively. They asked few questions.

The previous week, the party had scheduled 14 public meetings for the evening of Sunday March 11th. These meetings were planned as part of a blitz with an eye to elections. Bishop, Coard and Whiteman discussed in my presence the issue of whether the meetings should be postponed or not. They agreed that the meetings should go ahead. They felt that such a development would have Gairy guessing. They asked me to ensure that word to that effect was spread around the country. I asked them who would be the speakers at those meetings. They said that party activists would have to speak.

Bishop then gave me a slip of paper. He told me that I must take that paper to a certain rent-a-car business owner and obtain a car. He told me that if I was approached by the police, that I should eat the slip.

Twelve of the 14 planned public meetings were successfully accomplished. Young party activists throughout the country addressed thousands of people. The common theme of those meetings was 'fight back!'

Among the speakers on the night were Ian St. Bernard and Rudolph Ogilvie, both NLA members. They would both soon become heroic combatants of March 13th 1979.

St. Bernard was an effervescent personality. He was one of the revolutionaries who came through the ranks of OREL. He was always positive, totally committed and, in those unforgettable days leading up to the March 13th triumph, his every moment of existence had but one purpose – the liberation of Grenada!

Besides being an NLA member, St. Bernard was one of the leaders of the NJM youth arm and one of the leading publicists in the party.Because of his talent with the pen, he wrote articles for many of the party's publications.

Ogilvie was also a very serious type. Like Cornwall and St. Bernard, he was one of the young leaders in the St. Paul's community. He was one of the key persons involved in the production of the party's many newspapers and other publications. He was the radical type who was always ready to be in the front line of the fight against any manifestation of injustice. His enthusiasm earned him the sobriquet "Leftist" among his friends.

Chapter 11

Two-D Plan

On the night of March 11th I visited Bishop, Coard and Whiteman, for the third time in less than 12 hours. I informed them of the success of the meetings. They overflowed with pleasure.

It was clear that they had been discussing the question of launching the Revolution. I was able to pick that up from some of the things they said in my presence. But the leadership did not directly let me in on the nature of their discussions. At one point Coard said that it was necessary to implement the Two-D Plan.

"Two-D Plan?" I questioned myself. "What could that be?" I had never heard of it. But Bishop and Whiteman understood too well.

Finally they told me what the Two-D Plan was. It was a *deception* and *diversion* plan. It required the NLA to launch assaults at police stations and government installations around the country, except in St. George. I was told that the assaults were to be launched, and then the forces were to withdraw. No installation was to be entered. No weapons were to be seized. The twin objectives of these attacks were to deceive Gairy as to the tactics and capacity of the NLA, to lure him to

66

the view that the party was only capable of isolated hit and run strikes; and to force him to spread his forces islandwide to cover the many isolated targets, thereby diverting them from the real targets.

I was truly fascinated by the surpassing brilliance of the whole idea. Almost in a trance I rose to leave, to pass on instructions for the implementation of the plan. To think that I was cursing these men only a few days before. I smiled at the thought. As I was leaving, Bishop told me that I should not check them back; that they would contact me.

In the early hours of March 12th 1979, Molotov cocktails and small arms fire disrupted the sleep of Gairy's forces in a number of police stations around Grenada. The Two-D Plan was implemented. Cornwall, Ventour, one other person, and I greeted Revolution Eve by carrying out one such attack. D-Day minus one had arrived!

Chapter 12

We Move: Tonight!

At 8:30 on the morning of March 12th I left home in the company of my school friend, the same one who had contacted me the previous morning. That day was a workday, but Mathematics and Economics[16] were the furthest things from my mind. My father, observing that I made no preparation to go to work asked me what was the matter. I told him that because of the tense situation in the country I thought it unwise to travel to St. David. My white lie in place, I left to see the leadership. This time Bishop, Coard and Whiteman were hiding out in the North East St. George area. They had moved in there in the wee hours of the morning.

I remained with the leadership for about ninety minutes on this occasion. I informed them of the implementation of the Two-D Plan. They expressed subdued satisfaction. They seemed very pensive, tired and tense, clear effects of the stress of the last few days. When I joined them, they were in the process of discussing 'the Way Forward in the Present Situation,' a euphemism for 'Attack or no Attack?'.

Bishop and Whiteman expressed the view that the party was not yet ready to carry out the attack. They said that we did not have enough weapons; that it was unrealistic to attack Gairy's army of 200 men, backed up by 36 armed police stations, with only 60 men, 16 M-1 rifles, a few shotguns, a few revolvers and Molotov cocktails. They said that the position adopted previously, of holding off, should stand; and that Sello's [Selwyn Strachan's] mission should be given time to succeed.

They therefore expressed the view that the leadership should continue to lie low, and observe the direction things were taking. The two leaders felt that the situation was likely to cool off. Once the tense atmosphere cooled off, the leadership would be able to re-emerge publicly. The dangerous period of one year before when Belmar was assassinated was referred to. At that time the leadership went into hiding and was able to re-emerge after the situation returned to normal.

Coard on the other hand expressed the view that the time had come to move. He said that Gairy was intent on smashing the party and that he was going to use the Grease issue as the excuse and justification for so doing. He agreed that additional weapons would greatly enhance the chances of victory; but, he argued, that the party faced an immediate situation. In his opinion it would be a fatal error to wait. Coard agreed that it sounded crazy for 60 men to attack Gairy's army, but felt that such a 'crazy attack' would be the last thing that Gairy would look for. He expressed confidence that Gairy's forces would be 'surprised' and that the 'element of surprise' would make the 'crazy idea' a success in reality.

"Indeed!" I said to myself as I listened, "Not only Gairy would be surprised."

Right there and then I was receiving a complete surprise; shock is the more appropriate term. Here was Bernard Coard the 'perfectionist' who only weeks before portrayed himself as a paragon of caution, a stickler for detail; Bernard Coard who had placed obstacle after obstacle in the way of launching the attack; Bernard Coard whose 'cowardice' it seemed to me could not adequately be described by all the expletives in the English language – here was this Bernard Coard right in front of my very eyes arguing fervently for an immediate move. It all seemed unreal.

It was then and only then I understood what was happening: all along the top leadership had been split on the question of moving. Coard's string of excuses and new demands were all stalling tactics. It was this split which had kept Gairy in power for the last few weeks. The lack of radio communications, the imprecision of details, the mock-ups for practice were all red herrings.

There had been an insistence among the leadership that more weapons and more men were needed before the attack could be carried out. That position had won out. As a result, NJM Political Bureau member Selwyn Strachan was sent on a mission to Cuba in an effort to obtain additional weapons. Strachan's cover for going to Cuba was that of attending an international students' meeting being held in Cuba at the time.

Although my main form of participation in the discussion was by way of listening, I was given the opportunity to reiterate my personal position and what I knew to be the position of the leading NLA members – Move!

To move forward, Coard suggested that I should go and contact Ventour and find out if he had any latest information from 'Patsy' of Gairy's latest intentions. 'Patsy' was an agent in the police who reported to the party through Ventour. 'Patsy' had a line to the highest levels of Gairy's security apparatus, and a history of providing very reliable information. As such it was agreed by the three senior leaders of the party that feedback from 'Patsy' would help the leadership to arrive at a decision on the way forward.

Within fifteen minutes, I located Ventour who was in an excited mood. He had startling information. And for over one hour he had been making frantic efforts to contact me. 'Patsy' had contacted him about 9:00 a.m. and told him that Gairy was leaving the country around 2:00 p.m. for a period of one week. Gairy had instructed his top security officials that on his return, he wanted to see either the graves[17] or the cells[18] of Bishop, Coard, Whiteman and Austin. The situation was clearly urgent and grave.

I rushed back to inform the leadership of the situation. When I told them the information from 'Patsy', they were stunned. Bishop leaned back his head and stared at the roof drawing in heavily on his cigarette at the same time. Coard stood up and began walking around the room, in a seemingly aimless manner. Whiteman cupped his hands, and bowed his head into it. A completely new complexion was now cast on the situation.

It was Coard who spoke first. "Comrades, we cannot delay! We must move!" He spoke for over 30 minutes, but not quite 45.

Bishop as usual listened attentively with only intermittent interjections. As he listened he held a pen in his hand and made nervous scratches on a piece of paper in front of him. Whiteman continuously and nervously took off his glasses, wiped them, put them back on, and then performed the same ritual all over again.

Coard as he spoke made an analysis of the situation in Grenada, the Caribbean region, the USA and the wider world. He expressed the view that a revolutionary situation existed in Grenada. He said that the Grenadian masses had reached a stage where they were not prepared to continue being ruled in the old way; that they were desperate for change; that the pressure on them was too much, and they could take it no longer! This he said had led to a situation where Gairy and his ruling clique were forced to shift gears in order to maintain their hold on power. He also said that the growing strike movement and militancy of the working class in particular and the masses in general, the intense political activity of NJM amongst the masses, the economic collapse and worsening social conditions, which daily aggravated the situation, had all led to growing political opposition; that the opposition had reached a level where Gairy could continue to control the situation only by escalating (yet further) his reign of repression; and that escalation was about to take the form of the physical elimination of the leadership of the party.

All this he stressed had led to heightened antagonism in the society, with a people desperate for change and increasingly becoming active in the struggle for such change versus a dictatorship equally determined to hold on at all costs including murdering its political opponents. Coard said that it was because of this desperation by the people for change, combined with their unbending conviction that Gairy could never ever be moved by a ballot box, which he controlled, that the masses had reacted with such cynicism and contempt when party members had approached them in the last week with talk of elections. He said it was as a result of this situation party members had received the response – "Roll out the Grease!" from the masses.

And, Coard further reasoned, given their mood the people would answer the call of the party and hit the streets to complete the overthrow of Gairy, once the NLA routed the Green Beast.

Coard also integrated the impact of the party's organisational work into his analysis. He said that the organisational work of the party over the past few years had resulted in the building of the party machine of 5000 Grenadians; that this provided the masses with a revolutionary vanguard which would enable them to undertake organised and efficient revolutionary action to ensure that the dictatorship could not get up once it was floored.

Furthermore, Coard reasoned that the moment was ripe to move not only because the masses were ready, but also because they would be up against a ruling clique which was at its weakest. He pointed out that the ruling class in Grenada had been for some time split into two wings; and that a bitter feud had persisted within that class with Gairy's consistent and concerted campaign to crush the wing comprised of the old ruling class elements. That bitter feud, he said, had resulted in a situation in which the old elements of the ruling class had become convenient allies of the people in the anti-Gairy struggle. Therein, Coard argued, lay the significance of the People's Alliance – the parliamentary opposition. This split in the ruling class greatly weakened the strength of the forces that would be ready to resist revolutionary action.

Coard also said that Gairy, by his conduct in international circles, his growing links with latrine regimes as Chile and South Korea, and the effective exposure of his corruption and dictatorial practices, had developed an Idi Amin-buffoon type of image; and that had led to his isolation from the ruling circles in the imperialist countries – USA, UK, Canada – to the extent that they had refused to provide him with military assistance to deal with the internal situation. Thus Coard said that the 70% of the Grenadian masses and their vanguard – NJM – were up against a weakened Gairy, a Gairy and his ruling clique, isolated regionally and internationally and greatly weakened by constant and open struggle with the other wing of the ruling class. And that for those reasons he was at his weakest point and extremely vulnerable; hence it was the moment to decisively move in on him.

Coard further argued that Gairy's departure from the country was both good and bad. He said that his absence would mean that all the forces could be concentrated on Target Two – True Blue barracks; and that the problem of co-ordinating the actions in taking Target One and Target Two simultaneously would be eliminated. But he said that Gairy on the loose would be a dangerous quantity; that there would be the danger of him agitating his mass base from outside Grenada. At the time, the party estimated that despite Gairy's unpopularity, he had a hardcore mass base of 30% of the electorate. Coard said that Gairy might even attempt to mobilise a mercenary force to retake the country; therefore the tempo of actions to overthrow the dictatorship and consolidate internally would have to be intense and rapid; that the party would have to obtain assistance quickly in the form of weapons and training to rapidly build an army of the Revolution; and that immediate measures would have to be taken to woo Gairy's mass base, the heart of which was the approximately 2,000 agricultural workers and their families, with the objective of first neutralising them, and then winning them over to the side of the Revolution.

The balance of forces in the English-speaking Caribbean was favourable to a revolutionary uprising, Coard continued. Gairy was an embarrassment in the region, and he was isolated by all the other governments; that Manley and Burnham would immediately recognise a new government; that Burnham would immediately provide material assistance for the defence of the Revolution; and that Burnham and Manley would assist the Revolution to overcome any economic or political pressure which any of the other English-speaking Caribbean countries might attempt to exert on the new revolutionary government.

The Revolution would be viewed as a welcome development on the world scene, and the international situation was auspicious for the arrival of the Revolution, Coard further argued. He said that the world was experiencing a period of upsurge in the national liberation struggle; that the process had gained tremendous momentum with the victory of the Vietnamese revolutionaries in the Vietnam War; that the momentum was increased with the victories in Angola, Mozambique and other African nations; and that the attention of the world was then focused on the recently successful Iranian revolution, on developments in South East Asia and on the unfolding revolution in Nicaragua. Those developments, he said, had placed US imperialism on the defensive worldwide, and had occupied their attention. He stated that those developments, particularly the defeat sustained by US forces in Vietnam, combined with the Watergate scandal, had also brought on a changed mood inside the US; and that a non-interventionist mood was then dominant in the US. In that regard he analysed the significance of the congressional law prohibiting the US administration from providing assistance to the counter-revolutionary movement in Angola. For those reasons Coard said that he felt that the United States would not be of the mind to immediately intervene in Grenada to smash a successful revolution.

And, Coard said, even if the US government were of that mind, many objective problems would be faced in moving from desire to action. He pointed out that for decades the US had treated the English-speaking Caribbean region with what he called 'benign neglect'. As such, any revolution was bound to take them by complete surprise. And because of the upsurge in the world revolutionary movement the US was spread far and wide and occupied elsewhere; a factor which he said would facilitate a successful revolution, because on deeper analysis, the US would view Grenada as small game, not worth the effort of diverting forces and attention. Further, he said, the US lack of information on the Caribbean region, and lack of an apparatus in the region, results of US imperialism's neglect of the region, were bound to act as serious hindrances to immediate US intervention, if not make it impractical.

Coard said that, however, when all was said and done, a key factor in holding the hand of the imperialist world would be the initial moves of the Revolution. He said that once the initial pronouncements of the Revolution were not too radical, the Revolution would win the time and space necessary for consolidation.

The information from 'Patsy' and the brilliance, power and logic of Coard's discourse created an electric atmosphere. One could have felt that history was being decided. I felt truly honoured that the party leadership had the confidence in me to allow me to witness it.

When Bishop spoke, his voice carried a graveness and solemnity apt for the situation and decision at hand. His main concern was to ensure that the party did not take any premature and precipitate action, and thereby commit suicide. As party leader he carried a great personal weight and responsibility on his shoulders for the future of the party; its effects were manifest; it took on physical form as the pain of conflict showed up on his face. He raised the possibility of remaining in hiding for the period that Gairy would be out of the country, and then emerging after that. He expressed the view that Gairy's forces would not move violently on the leadership while he – Gairy – was in the country. He said that ever since the famous Duffus Commission of inquiry had implicated Gairy in the brutal acts of November 18th 1973 and January 21st 1974, Gairy nearly always ensured that he was out of the state whenever his forces were to carry out brutal and criminal acts. And, in true forensic style, Bishop produced a string of evidence to support his view.

Whiteman maintained his strong doubts about the feasibility of the NLA defeating Gairy's army. He too raised the option of remaining in hiding. Additionally, he said that if the situation got really hot, then the leadership together with the NLA could put up a fight from the hills. He said that at least the world would see that the party was acting in self-defence, against Gairy's fascist onslaught.

After over one hour of the highest quality discussion that I had ever heard in the party, or in the revolutionary struggle up until then, Coard suggested that the other members of the Political Bureau should be contacted, and called in to give their views.

Bishop agreed, but he added, "Of course Dix cannot be involved in this." He was referring to Kenrick Radix.

The party leadership had a policy of excluding Radix from all discussions, knowledge and involvement in military activities. I knew the reason for that policy. We NLA members were forewarned of the policy, lest someone out of naiveté, knowing that Radix was a Political Bureau member, should raise NLA affairs with him.

The story went that in 1974, at the height of the unsuccessful 1973-74 Revolution, the NJM, then less than one year old, had planned to move on Gairy. The matter was discussed and agreed on by the Bureau of which Radix was a member. Radix then, clearly motivated by love and concern for his family, unwisely informed his parents that an attack was to be carried out, and he advised them to go into hiding. Radix's family then apparently shared the information with friends, advising them likewise.

Grenada being Grenada, the planned attack was soon the most widely known secret in Grenada. Even well known Grenadian journalist, Alister Hughes, a staunch opponent of Gairy, gained possession of the information. By way of telephone, he contacted one of the leaders of the party for confirmation of this information. Obviously this was hot news!

With that leak, the only logical and correct decision was to call off the attack. It took only 24 hours for the party to know what a correct decision that was. It was the proverbial stitch in time. Gairy's forces had been waiting in ambush to massacre the Jewel attackers. Radix's indiscretion had almost caused a disaster.

However, in fairness to Radix, despite the near disaster resulting from his indiscretion, he continued to make significant contributions to the anti-Gairy struggle. His great strengths were his skills as an orator – he was one of the best in the party – and tremendous personal courage and militancy. He was a man for the platform, a man for the demonstration, a man to stand and face Gairy's terror forces. These strengths were invaluable during the days of the anti-Gairy struggle.

With past experience in mind, and undoubtedly taking his strengths into consideration, Bishop said that it would be best for Radix to leave the country and be based overseas at this critical moment. He instructed me to tell Radix that he must leave the same evening for Barbados. A conference had been planned in Barbados for March 13th with the US lawyer who was defending Humphrey and Wardally in the US. Bishop had been scheduled to attend the conference, but obviously he could not now make it. Thus there was a perfect and legitimate basis for sending Radix.

Bishop also instructed me to contact Austin and George Louison, and to lead them to join the meeting. Radix was informed as instructed. I contacted Phyllis Coard, who is also now on death row (1988), and asked her to contact George Louison. I told her to tell him that we would rendezvous at Bishop's home.

In St. Paul's, I met my friend Cornwall. Ventour and Gahagan were with him. Ventour had already relayed to them the information from 'Patsy'. They told me that Austin was also apprised of the situation. Together we visited Austin. Redhead was with him when we arrived at his hideout. I told him – Austin – that Maurice, Bernard and Whiteman were discussing the question of launching the attack against Gairy, and that he was needed to give his views. There was no need to settle collectively our position, for it was well known. And it was known that Austin's position of support for an immediate move on Gairy was rock firm! Indeed, in the last four months preceding March 13th his life had but one reason, one meaning, one purpose– the making of the Revolution! He had a strange way of referring to himself as 'the old man'. He was only 40 years old at the time. But somehow he had convinced himself that he had but a few more years of life. To hear him talk one would have believed that he was 70 years old.

"If we miss this boat then I would not see my dream come true," he continuously rued during the weeks of indecision. And like a man possessed, oblivious of night and day, divested of natural callings, for four full months, Comrade H.A., as he was fondly called, had worked, almost slaved, to bring his dream to reality. There was simply not a chance in a million that he would have voted against the New Jewel Movement and its National Liberation Army fulfilling their appointment with destiny.

However, because of the information from 'Patsy', we discussed whether it would not be better to launch the Revolution that same afternoon; to start by capturing Gairy on his way to the airport. The military comrades felt that it was possible to mount such an operation; to capture Gairy over the Grand Etang hills. Of course, this would have meant a fundamental alteration to the strategy previously settled on. Additionally, such an option meant that we would have had to operate under a serious time constraint. But still, we felt that if that was acceptable to the leadership then we were prepared to do it.

Dressed in a suit, felt hat and glasses, Austin entered the back seat of the car. His prominent beard was, by a few minutes, no more. His hair had been cut low, US Marine regulation style. Lester Redhead had done a good job in outfitting him with a new appearance. As he entered the car and settled, Austin was handed a newspaper that he held open in front of him. With his head slightly bent, he focused his eyes on the paper like a business executive completely taken up with the latest profit and loss statement of his company. Cornwall and I next entered the back seat on opposite sides of Austin. Gahagan, a mixture of confidence and nervous enthusiasm, was seated in the front seat. And Ventour, the expert driver, had control of the wheel. In a few minutes the efficacy of the disguise meticulously assembled by Austin and Redhead would be put to the test.

Ventour drove off. As he approached the police station we held our breath. Two policemen were standing in front of the police station. Ventour remained cool and drove impassively on. Austin kept his eyes stuck to the paper seemingly unaware of the tension-filled situation. Gahagan, Cornwall and I kept our heads slightly bowed.

We passed the police station. The policemen, unperturbed, maintained their position. They continued observing the traffic as it streamed by in both directions. And so, one of the four most wanted men in Grenada passed undetected under the nose of the police.

Ten minutes later Austin and I got out of the car. We had to walk one kilometre of unpopulated area to reach our destination.

As we entered the house, Bishop, Coard and Whiteman froze. Then together in genuine excitement they laughed. They too had failed to recognise Austin until he removed his hat.

Within ten minutes of his arrival, and after Bishop, Coard and Whiteman had outlined their positions to him, Austin cast his vote. Move! The scorecard now read two for, two against, or more accurately, two doubtful. Only one vote was still outstanding – George Louison's. The other two members of the leadership with a right to vote were unavailable. Selwyn Strachan was in Cuba, and Vincent Noel was in police custody.

By then though, it was clear that the option of seizing Gairy on his way to the airport and commencing the Revolution from then, was not viable. And hence the matter was only fleetingly discussed.

At approximately 2:30 p.m. I met George Louison at the rendezvous. We quickly covered the few kilometres to the hiding place of the top leaders of the NJM. We had one scare along the way. In a secluded area, we unexpectedly came across a farmer grazing a flock of sheep. We became really concerned when we realised who the farmer was. He was a former Superintendent of Police. We were not prepared for such an encounter. Louison told the former policeman that we had lost a cow, and we were looking for it. It was a totally implausible story; but it was better than no story, I suppose. The former policeman clearly unconvinced told us that he had not observe any cow in the area. We then made a detour. Observing closely to ensure that we were not being followed we went back on course and made it to the location where Bishop and the others were. We were, I thought, minutes away from the Decision.

We Move Tonight

But that was not to be: before any serious discussion took place, Bishop said, "I think that Bogo and Aki should be called in to participate in the discussion." He was referring to Leon 'Bogo' Cornwall and Basil 'Aki' Gahagan.

"You are wanted," I told Gahagan and Cornwall, as I met them in the St. Paul's area. "Not by the police ... by the Revolution!" I added to inject a little drama. They were clearly delighted by the news that they were summoned to join the discussions. The sense of esteem they felt was written all over their faces. The spring in their strides, as we hurried to join history, was worth a million words. They were on their way to not only witness but, to an extent, to participate in a historic decision.

But I was not to witness the moment of decision. Before we could get into any discussion, Bishop suggested that I should again leave to contact Ventour. This I did. It was during that hour while I was out that the Decision was taken. The story of that moment I have heard many times. But an eyewitness far better tells it. As I write, my friend Leon Cornwall is located a few cells away from me. He is speaking to me now.

He says, "Maurice said that they wanted our views, Aki's and my views, on the way forward. In the room were Maurice, Bernard, Uni, H.A. and George Louison. I remember that the atmosphere was electrifying – a sort of air of expectancy came from each of them. It came across as if they wanted our views so as to finally decide what should be done. They gave no indication of any differences in positions among the Political Bureau members; and up until then I did not know of any differences. To me it seemed that they were seeking out my and Aki's views to decide if we were psychologically ready to die if necessary, to liberate the land from Gairyism. Since Aki and I were to play key roles in the attack, I saw it as the acid test. There could be no other reason, for our position was well known. But it's said that the critical moment proves the true man, and there could have been no moment more critical than that moment of decision.

"I can't remember who spoke first, whether Aki or myself, but I remember that my whole attitude was one as if that was a normal, natural and welcome development. Only one thought pervaded my mind – 'We have to move Gairy, and move him tonight!'

"I stated clearly and briefly to Maurice that we must make the hit that very night!

"He asked some questions about the psychological state of the other leading NLA members. Both Aki and I stated emphatically that the comrades were all ready, eager, and willing to move right away. And that because of the constant postponements, some were even questioning whether the party was serious.

"He asked whether we felt that we could really deal with Gairy's Green Beast. Aki said that the surprise element was the main thing. He said that we would have that going for us, because they [Green Beast] felt that they had us on the run, and so they won't expect us to lash them. I pointed out to Maurice that just a few days before, H.A. and I had personally made a recce [reconnaissance] in True Blue on the Green Beast barracks, and that I felt we could deal with them, because even though tension was high in the country, the last thing that they were expecting was a move on them.

"I think that Bernard asked some questions, testing our positions. I believe that he was trying to see how resolute we were in our position, a kind of devil's advocate role. He asked things like: 'Are you two comrades sure that you can mobilise enough men who are psychologically prepared to fight to the last? Do you realise that once we move, we can't turn back, and that we might fail and die?'

"To me failure was really the last thing in my mind, since I was convinced that we could win. Both Aki and I responded that 'Yes, we may have to die, but we are convinced that we will win.'

"After some more testing questions, Bernard said, 'What is your position, Aki: we move or we don't move?'

"Aki answered, 'We must move – tonight!'

"Bernard then said, 'And you Bogo?'

"I said, 'We must move – tonight!'

"With that Bernard said in a sort of half-questioning, half-conclusive voice: 'Well comrades, we move tonight?'

"And with that everybody – Maurice, Bernard, Uni, the General, George, Aki and myself – spontaneously joined hands together, like children playing ring-a-ring-a-roses, in one big hand shake. This was the unambiguous indication that we were all united in one agreement to smash Gairyism by armed struggle from that very night.

"Then both Maurice and Bernard gave us some pep talk on the need to go all out; that fearless determination was the most important thing; and that we were about to liberate our country in a history-making event, and we must feel proud and honoured to be in the vanguard of that struggle. They both made me feel that was the most supreme moment of my life. I must say that I did not experience any emotion of fear or doubt. My one thought was of victory.

"After that Maurice said, 'Well comrades, you have work to do.' He gave me a hand written note and told me to bring this to a certain man in St. David. He told me to introduce myself with the words 'We want the printing press' and then give him the note. And he said that I must do whatever the man told me to do."

I arrived back just before Cornwall departed. Ventour and I were informed that the decision was 'Go'.

It was the vote of George Louison which had clinched the decision in the Political Bureau. His support for the position of moving was stated before Cornwall and Gahagan entered the meeting. Thus the decision to move had been agreed on by the Bureau. However, it was finally settled by the political and military leaders of the party.

In turns, we NLA members departed to carry out our task of mobilising men and weapons for the attack. As we left we embraced the leaders of the party. We thought then that we were seeing them for the last time in a Grenada under the heels of dictatorship.

Chapter 13

Freedom Hill

There is a Hill in the southern end of Grenada, in the area of Lance Aux Epines. A Hill which today stands guard over the southern tip of the island which contains the International Airport, the greatest monument of the brief but productive reign of the Revolution. From that Hill, the azure waters of the Caribbean Sea carry on a romance with the eyes. And that unique mix of fresh sea breeze and the reflection of the sun's rays from the mirror-like Grand Anse Beach, which many rate as the greatest creation of its type, produce pure bliss to the human senses. Freedom Hill, as it is called, is arguably the symbolic peak of Grenada's History. There, 46 Grenadians, most of them less than 25 years old, gathered in the waning hours of March 12th 1979. And even before the March 13th dawn announced its presence, they descended that Hill and swept the Gairy dictatorship off the Grenadian landscape.

Fittingly, during the years of the Revolution, on every seventh day of February, Grenadian youths celebrated the anniversary of the attainment of independence from Britain, by marching all of the 30 miles from Leapers' Hill, in the northernmost part of Grenada, to Freedom Hill. In this way they marched not only the entire physical length of Grenada, but also the entire history, until then, of the struggle for freedom in Grenada.

Leapers' Hill is the location in the north of the island where Caribs – original inhabitants of Grenada – were massacred by French colonisers in 1650. The massacre was an act of revenge by the French for heroic Carib resistance to French efforts to steal their lands and conqueror them[19]. And Freedom Hill, we hoped, would become the Hill from which the last dictator was swept from Grenada. It took approximately 329 years to travel those 30 miles!

And indeed, as we gathered on Freedom Hill for a few historic hours, we were conscious that we carried in our breasts the dreams and hopes and aspirations of four centuries; that we were simply the anchor-leg carrying the torch in a long relay of human struggle. For as long as my heart cares to beat, I will remember those brief hours of Freedom Hill, and those which followed shortly thereafter.

Chapter 14

Mobilisation

I arrived at Freedom Hill just before March 12th surrendered to March 13th. After leaving Bishop and the other political and military leaders, I proceeded to St. George. There I saw my friend Liam Owusu James. The police had released him only hours before. I informed him of the decision to move. I told him that he should mobilise his men. And I promised to get back to him.

Then I headed in the direction of St. Paul's. I was on my way to the home of Strachan Phillip. On the route I met a friend of mine from Presentation College days.

"Ache! What is the scene, man?" he said in a voice, a mixture of excitement, relief and confusion. "Ache, I'm in trouble, real trouble man. Ah hear the police looking for me to question me on this grease business."

He went on to explain to me that as part of his job of clearing imports from Customs for a St. George firm, he had cleared several barrels of grease. He said that was over six months ago. Now, he said, he understood that the police were saying that those were the barrels in which Jewel brought in the guns. As a result they were looking for him to question him, as part of the investigations to recover the contents of the barrels. He said that he did not know what he would tell the police, and so he wanted my advice.

"Watch, doh dig nothing; just lie low and nothing go come out ah dat," I said to him. And without waiting to hear more, I moved on, leaving him there, his confusion compounded.

As I entered Strachan Phillip's home, I saw him sitting in the kitchen.

"Let's take a little walk," I said to him, greetings omitted. "I have something to show you." He rose and we walked out into the yard. "Phillip, the moment has arrived. Gairy is spending his last hours in power. We move, tonight!" I said to him, announcing the decision to move.

"Oh no, Layne! You like to tease me too much. You not joking, nah?" he asked with his arms opened, desperately wanting it to be true yet cannot believing it to be true.

He had taken the disappointment of postponement after postponement of the attack very badly. And even though we were all disappointed and demoralised, we sometimes eased the pressure by making small talk and small jokes about those constant delays.

"No, Phillip, I'm serious. We are moving."

"Oh God, Layne! These are the words I have wanted to hear all my fucking life. It's not true! It's not true! I don't fucking believe it!! After all these years of tears, of weeping, of suffering, Grenadians will wake up tomorrow with a smile on their face."

"Shrrr!" I said to him in an effort to quieten him down.

By this time he was almost hysterical. There were people inside, and the house was near to the road, so I was afraid that others would hear him. As he cooled down completely, his face gradually regaining the appearance of normalcy, coming to grips with the news I gave him, I said, "Phillip, we have to be on the Hill by midnight."

He knew where I meant by 'The Hill'. Austin and Redhead and other apostles had led training courses in that area; and the engineering firm of which Austin was a partner was involved in the construction of roads in the same area. Phillip had visited the area on a number of occasions, though he never participated in any of the training sessions held there. He used to laugh and say that he was too much of an expert with weapons for any man to teach him how to use a gun.

"I will therefore like you to lend me your jeep," I continued, "to go to St. David. In the meantime you should mobilise your men and any weapons you have. When I return we will leave for the Hill."

"OK, Layne, any fucking thing you say. You expect me not to help out a bird that brings good news?" he said, amidst much laughter.

I left for St. David in the company of an NLA member who was a friend of mine for many years, going back to primary school days. The St David area was unusually busy. Police vehicles were patrolling up and down the street. It was an obvious response to the NLA's attack in the area the previous night. The effects of the Two-D Plan were indeed pervasive. Yet, as I think back, we were neither afraid nor concerned.

In St. David we collected a few weapons from different locations. However, we experienced difficulties in mobilising the NLA members in the area. We were able to mobilise only three NLA members. We decided that only two would accompany us to participate in the initial assault, and that the third NLA member would remain in the area to lead the mobilisation of additional forces, after the Green Beast were routed.

On my way back to St. George, I stopped off for a short while at the home of the woman I was in love with at the time, and who is the mother of my daughter. As I entered the house she ran to me shouting "Ewart! Ewart, my dear, where have you been all day? I was trying to get in touch with you. Ewart, I'm so worried."

"Why are you worried?" I replied, sidestepping the question, and addressing her concern. "You know there is no need to worry. You know I can take care of myself, not so?"

"That is true. But ... things are so tense, Ewart. And I know ... You are ... you are so committed." She was obviously not reassured.

I held her close to me. Before I could say anything more, I saw the question in her eyes, a question, which quickly changed to fear.

"Hold this," I said, as I handed her a bracelet that belonged to me. "Hold this," and I handed her a chain, which her mother had given her as a birthday present and which in turn she had given to me.

Then I said, "I owe Mrs. Sylvester some money. At the end of the month, I would like you to collect my salary, and pay her for me."

This was my small diversionary plan, but I was also taking measures to pay the people, at whom I lived in St. David, just in case I died. I also knew that by speaking of the end of the month, I would throw her off. She would feel that maybe I was going off to some unknown and unnamed place. It would not have been the first time that I would have done such a thing.

Then with my eyes locked on her, I said, "Maureen, if anything ever happens to me," a smooth euphemism for the unmentionable 'if I die', "and you have a son, would you name him after me?"

"Oh yes, my dear," she answered.

"Promise?" I asked, opening my hands and tilting my head to the right, to emphasise the request.

"Yes! Promise," she replied.

With that we embraced, and for a few minutes we kissed into eternity. I was conscious that it could well have been our last kiss, but somehow it did not seem to matter. As I turned to leave, she said, "Hold this," and smiling she placed back the chain around my neck.

Matters of the heart fully settled, I then proceeded back down for St. George.

At the home of Strachan Phillip, it was quite a scene. I met Phillip in his dining room, his two feet up on the table, and a bottle of rum in front of him. He was there with about eight others. He sang. He drank. He chatted. He cursed.

"Gairy, you son of a bitch! Tonight is your last! Green Beast here I come, start to run; I've blood in my eyes!" he said over and over again, as he laughed and cried himself to hysteria.

About 11:00 p.m., I said, "Phillip, I think we should be moving."

"Anything you say, Layne, anything you say." And amazingly he switched back to a state of apparent sobriety. After a short pause he said, "Boys, let's get moving."

We left the area in Phillip's jeep. There were about 15 of us in the jeep. And we had about five weapons with us. We passed directly in front of one of Gairy's main police stations. As I sit and recollect now, I realise that that was one hell of a chance. But at the time though, there seemed nothing chancy about it. We had a duty, and we were simply carrying it out. And so with a brief stop by my home, we were on our way to Freedom Hill.

Chapter 15

Combat Order

And to Freedom Hill they all came. From St. John came Einstein Louison with a group, and with weapons. Basil Gahagan brought men from as far as St. Mark and as close as St. George. John Chalky Ventour came along with men from North East St. George. Redhead brought additional men from South East St. George. And some men also came from South St. George. Forty-six men at the final count. Among them was Keith Hayling, a young Insurance Salesman who four and a half years later would be killed in the October 19th tragedy. David Lambert then, as me, a mere 20 years old, was also there. He would later become a popular medical doctor and sadly succumb to cancer in the prime of his life. Before that final count there were 50 combatants but four slipped out, considering the whole scheme harebrained.

There were urban workers, farmers, teachers, professionals, skilled workmen, small-businessmen and unemployed; a high proportion being youth. The varied social and class background of the 46 combatants was illustrative of the broad social forces allied against the dictatorship and indicative of the party's broad links in the society. But there were no agricultural workers. And this was a manifestation of the nascent state of the party's work among that strata; and the fact that Gairy still had a strong hold on that them, despite the signs of cracks.

We sat together. We talked. We joked. We laughed. "Shrrr," Austin or Gahagan would say regularly, indicating the need for silence. And for a moment the decibel level would go down slightly; and then it would rise again. Finally, the only solution was to split up into small groups. It was impossible to bring an end to the talking. We all wanted to talk, to express in words our mind's possessions.

We talked about the moon, which shone with exceptional brilliance. About the many stars. About the breeze. About the sinuous beauty of Freedom Hill. About our loved ones. About our past adventures, and future aspirations. For once, there was no 'no go area'. Nothing was taboo. And to sum it all up, the Poet Cornwall rendered a few words from a magnificent poem symbolising the passing away of dictatorship and the birth of the Revolution.

About 2:00 a.m. there was a small flourish. We saw figures ascending the Hill. Suddenly, everyone went quiet. Tension enveloped the hill. The sound of the cool breeze became audible. Weapons were drawn. "Apple", a voice called out, as we waited ready to spring into action. "Juice", came the response. It was an unmistakable voice so friendly and so powerful that it instantly dissolved the tension. "Comrade Bish," some said; "Brother Bish," others said; "Maurice," still others said. To our great surprise Bishop, Coard, Whiteman and Louison were on the scene. The word of their presence passed very quickly. Most of us moved forward to greet the leaders of the party, and the future leaders of the Revolution. It was a surprise, a pleasant surprise. We had not expected them. We knew that it was dangerous for them to travel to Freedom Hill. But here they were, standing before us. They had arrived by a car that Bishop had organised for that purpose. They dropped off at the bottom of the Hill and the car proceeded, on the understanding that the driver would park it by the

Calabash Hotel, a few hundred metres away, and return to Freedom Hill on foot.

Bishop, his face beaming with a 20-carat smile, so dazzling that it contended with the moon for dominance, asked, "Is everything all right? Everybody happy? Ready to free the homeland?"

"Yeah," was the reply to each question. A restrained yeah, but one of profound meaning.

Greetings and introductions completed, Bishop then proceeded to rap with us for a few minutes. He said that the party leadership had decided that the hour had come to get rid of Gairy by force of arms. That it was a decision of great moment. And that the leadership was united in the decision. He ended with the words: "Victory is a Must!"

Then Coard took over. "How many men present?"

"Fifty, including you four," Gahagan answered.

"Are they organised into squads as yet?"

"Yes," Gahagan said, disingenuously, obviously trying to avoid a lecture from Coard.

"Who are the squad leaders?" ... One minute passed. Two minutes passed. No answer.

"Who are the squad leaders?" Coard repeated. Another minute passed. "Weapons and everything else present?" Coard asked. And without waiting for an answer he led a group aside. That group comprised Bishop, Whiteman, Louison, Austin, Gahagan and Cornwall. Cornwall told me after: "Bernard just unreeled the computer and started to go through a checklist of men, weapons, quantity of ammunition, quantity of Molotov cocktails ..."

It was from this count that we realised that Liam Owusu James and his unit were not present. I had completely forgotten to make arrangements to pick up James and his men.

John Chalky Ventour had left for St. George to pick up James. He first passed by the home of Victor Husbands and picked him up. Victor Husbands was a small businessman from the area of St. Paul's but lived in the south of the island in the Belmont area. He was a very active member of the NLA and, in his late fifties, he was the oldest of the 46 persons who carried out the attack.

Husbands had already been notified so he was waiting to be picked up. After one toot of the horn he emerged from his home and entered the car.

Ventour together with Husbands then proceeded in the direction of the Town of St. George. However, the area was buzzing with police activity as police patrols moved up and down. As a result, Ventour and Husbands considered that it was not worth the risk to go into St. George and so they returned to Freedom Hill. Thus did Liam Owusu James miss the March 13th appointment.

By the time Ventour arrived back things had begun to take on a more organised form. When the count was taken, we established that we had only 25 weapons. This was fewer than we hoped for. The Grease-famed 16 M-1 rifles formed part of these twenty-five weapons. But there were scores of Molotov cocktails.

Soon squads were organised. Squad One: Austin; Squad Two: Gahagan; Squad Three: Cornwall; Squad Four: Layne; Squad Five: Redhead. Then the chain of command – Overall Command: Austin; Second in Command: Gahagan; Third in Command: Cornwall.

However, there was intense discussion and struggle among the political and military leaders, before the structure of the Unit was established. The bone of contention was the question of the role of the leadership. The leadership expressed the view that they should be allowed to participate directly in the act of storming the True Blue barracks.

But Austin, Gahagan and Cornwall would have none of it. They argued that the 25 men with the best military training should be the ones to bear weapons. Therefore, for a start it meant that the four Political Bureau members would have to carry cocktails. Then they argued that four additional men carrying cocktails – not to mention untrained men (though out of deference this point was only implied) would make little difference to the outcome of the assault. Gahagan, in particular, rolling out the all-military position, argued that the place of the leadership was not on the front line, but at a suitable location some distance away, from where they could oversee things.

The fact of the shortage of weapons alone was enough to seal the issue; but it was prolonged. George Louison in particular was very upset by the exclusion of the leadership from direct participation in the main assault. He had turned up on Freedom Hill fully prepared for battle. He was dressed in his boots, and fatigue-type clothing. He had even secured a shotgun and a supply of ammunition to go with it. And now his weapon was to be taken away from him. He did not care whether he was equipped with a rifle, a shotgun, a pistol, cocktail or stone, he simply wanted a direct part in routing the Green Beast. Finally, though still disappointed, he gave in to the unyielding position of the military comrades.

After the structure of the unit was settled, the command group went to a higher point on Freedom Hill. Cornwall told me that they went up there to examine a route. The idea was mooted that it would be better to move from Freedom Hill to True Blue on foot. The intense police patrol of the area created a concern that if the NLA contingent moved by transport then they could become engaged before reaching True Blue. Secondarily there was the concern that the movement into True Blue of several vehicles at the same time could alert the Green Beast and result in the loss of the element of surprise. However, proceeding on foot had serious disadvantages. It would have entailed passing through a semi-jungle area.

Cornwall said, "When Bernard heard what was being contemplated he went mad. He conjured up scenes of men sticking in the swamp, falling over into ravines, damaging legs, and the unit still being in the bush by 8:00 a.m. We knew he was overstating it, but say what, you know Bernard; he had a point and he piled it on. Five minutes after everyone had agreed with him, he was still lecturing to win over the converted."

To finally settle the issue, however, it was decided that Ventour should go to True Blue and drive through the camp to check the state of alertness of the Green Beast soldiers. Remarkably the camp housing Gairy's soldiers was located in an unrestricted area and vehicles were allowed to pass through, to and fro, at all hours of day and night, unimpeded.

Ventour made the relatively short journey to True Blue. As he passed he observed only the usual one guard on duty; and this guard seemed more interested in the coolness of the weather than in anything Ventour was up to: he took no special notice of him. The Green Beast soldiers were clearly cocksure of their situation. Nowhere in their wildest imaginations could that guard and the other soldiers have perceived that they were an hour or so away from being routed.

Once Ventour reported back, the way was clear. The original idea to go to True Blue by means of transport was finally settled on. And the command group descended the hill back to the area where the unit was gathered.

Gahagan then called the remaining squad leaders and the rest of the unit together. We formed a circle around him and the other members of the Command group. Gahagan laid down some sticks on the ground. And he began explaining the scheme of the attack.

"You men only wasting fucking time!" Strachan Phillip bursted into the centre of the circle shouting. He kicked down the sticks. "This is simple mann. We just go in there and we start fucking shooting." Gahagan re-assembled his sticks. Phillip kicked them down again, "This is fucking shit mann! We have a job to do mann!"

"OK, OK," Bishop said, "take it away Phillip."

This incident summed up the idiosyncratic nature of Strachan Phillip. He was not always easy to get along with, but there was never a dull moment around him; and, undoubtedly, he was a man with a profound passion for freedom bordering on a disdain for rules.

Gahagan and Austin, without the aid of the sticks, then proceeded to explain the scheme of the attack.

Gahagan said, "We will leave this area by way of transport and drive straight to the True Blue barracks. Squad Two under my command will be the spearhead of the attack. We will drive right up, attack the guards and disarm them. Then we will move and occupy the high ground covering the main exit from the barracks. The rest of the Unit will disembark simultaneously and move for the high ground.

"Then from the high ground above the barracks we will concentrate fire on the barracks. Molotov cocktails will be simultaneously used to burn down the barracks. This is a very important part of the mission. The objective is to create maximum shock and panic to cause the Green Beast to flee in a disorganised state.

"The rate of fire and the unfolding situation will be directed and controlled by the command of Commander Austin. I will be the Second in Command on the attack and Cornwall will be next in line.

"Any questions?"

There were very few questions. Gahagan, who was a military fanatic, had done an excellent job in outlining the scheme of the attack.

Even today, as I look back from the vantage point of greater military experience and knowledge, I cannot but be impressed with the Plan itself, and how it was outlined. The Plan was clear, simple and creative – hallmarks of any good

Combat Order; and it was outlined with a sense of authority and conviction.

When Gahagan finished outlining the plan of attack, it was approaching 4:00 a.m.

Chapter 16

To Conquer or To Die

"Let's move, men," Austin ordered. And in a rush we descended Freedom Hill. The political leadership also descended the Hill. We jumped into a jeep and three cars. We were on our way to True Blue. We waved to Bishop and the others as we left. They themselves were waiting for their car to collect them to take them to an Observation Point a few hundred metres away from True Blue.

We drove out of the Lance Aux Epines area, past the popular Sugar Mill night club, and down 900 metres of stretch (now renamed the Maurice Bishop Highway). We bypassed the road leading to the front entrance of True Blue, and drove on to the Calliste road (which now leads to the Maurice Bishop International Airport) for a few hundred metres.

Then the first vehicle, a car driven by Chalky Ventour and occupied by Victor Husbands and two brothers, wheeled left moving off the main road into a side road; the other vehicles followed; and simultaneously all lights went off. We had crossed the Rubicon. The 'die was cast!'

We Move Tonight

We drove on, and on, to the edge of the world, to eternity, it seemed. We entered a zone with overhanging trees blocking out the moonlight. Emerging from this eerie zone, the moon lavished its brilliance on us. We went past the Radio Grenada Transmitter. A guard cloaked from head to foot, his countenance weighed down by the conflict between sleep and duty, peered through a window. Then as though rising out of the ground the edifice of the St. George's University School of Medicine appeared before us. We were almost there – to conquer or to die!

I glimpsed at my watch; it showed 4.15 a.m. We were entering True Blue from behind. It was a brilliant manoeuvre.

Bishop and his companions watched the cars with the combatants leave. They realised that neither the driver of their car, nor their car, were anywhere around. They waited a few minutes in the faint hope that the driver had left to collect the car, without forewarning them. But that hope quickly evaporated, as it dawned on them that they were stranded. Hastily the four men, three of them wanted dead or alive, hurried away on foot. As they made their way, dogs in the area erupted in uproar and attacked them. With sticks and stones they persuaded the dogs to retreat and then they started to run. They made it to the home of a strong supporter of the party. They pounded the bedroom window seeking urgent entry. And in a few minutes they were safely inside.

Chapter 17

The Battle

Bang! Bang! Bang! Rifle fire erupted in True Blue, sounding the clarion call of the Grenada Revolution.

Rapidly we disembarked from the vehicles, and leapt for the high ground. Bang! Bang! Bang! Rifle fire continued. Pah! Pah! Pah! Pah! Small arms joined in. Then from the vantage point of the high ground all weapons were unleashed. A cacophony of sounds, as diverse, yet as sweet as the early birds announcing the dawning day, filled the True Blue air.

Whoosh! A ball of fire erupted. Then another. Then another. As a group of young combatants, many of them no more than teenagers, armed with nothing else but Molotov cocktails, with the efficiency of machines, delivered their goods into the True Blue barracks. As they operated one could literally see sweat forming the letters of the word COURAGE down their young faces. And the barracks blazed, as if nature had defied its habits, and the sun itself had descended on True Blue barracks to rise up with splendour.

"Come out with your hands in the air! Come out with your hands in air!" the voice of Austin thundered above the many contending noises.

In response, Gairy's soldiers, taking advantage of the brief lull in the fire heaved out the windows. Naked, they raced through the bushes. More effective than a bulldozer, they made tracks through the thick briar trees surrounding the camp. And they bolted.

"Forward!" Austin thundered on. "Move in for the kill!" he bellowed as the aroma of victory filled the air.

One kilometre away, Bishop and his companions were observing the rising sun over True Blue. Coard rushed to the phone; he dialled the number seven and then three other numbers. Within minutes he was speaking to party activist Caldwell Taylor in St. Andrew.

"Caldwell, we have moved! True Blue barracks is on fire! Mobilise all forces in St. Andrew and move on the Grenville police station!!!"

Within twenty minutes Coard made one dozen such calls to mobilise the party network and the NLA islandwide.

"Forward!" Austin thundered on. We moved in. Prisoners were tied up.

"Squad Four, take the armoury!" Austin ordered.

We rushed in the direction of the armoury. Boom! An explosion went off. The suffocating scent of tear gas enveloped the armoury. We rushed back out. In the excitement one of our men had accidentally fired a gas grenade from a gas gun into the armoury.

"Surround the camp! Surround the camp!" Austin continued shouting orders. And smoothly, and with a level of organisation and discipline belying our inexperience, we completed the task of defeating, dispersing, disarming Gairy's Green Beast, and heralding the Grenada Revolution. It took forty-five minutes to secure the area. In that time, the NLA sustained no deaths or injuries. Gairy's Green Beast sustained no losses. We allowed them to flee in panic – only two were taken prisoner. All the squads had accomplished their missions; and the weapons worked well.

But even before we left True Blue, we had occasion to enjoy a laugh at Strachan Phillip's expense. When he attempted to send off his first shot, his rifle jammed. It required a very simple corrective measure, but he did not know how to carry it out. He had missed all the classes! In anger he smashed it on the ground. Only after we gathered the weapons from the Green Beast did he get another rifle.

With True Blue secured, Austin selected Strachan Phillip, Redhead, another person and me to go with him to capture Radio Grenada. We left Gahagan in charge of the rest of the unit at True Blue, with instructions to move to Radio Grenada once the area was fully mopped up.

Capturing Radio Grenada proved a very simple mission, for security was weak at that location. We drove right up to the entrance, got out of the vehicle and discharged our weapons in the air.

Austin shouted out, "Lay down your weapons and come out with your arms in the air!" The guards dropped their weapons, scaled a ten-foot fence and fled.

Inside Radio Grenada we knocked in the doors of the different rooms to make sure there were no guards hiding anywhere. And then my stupidity born of the dizziness of victory took control of me. Whack! I assaulted a glass-framed picture of the dictator. I jumped back in disbelief as blood spilled from my hand. What a fool I was!

Within minutes of taking over Radio Grenada a car approached. We took up defensive positions. The car door opened. "Apple! Apple! Apple!" There was no mistaking it. It was the excited voice of Bishop shouting the password.

"Juice!" Austin responded. And then Bishop, Coard, Whiteman and Louison rushed forward. Bishop and the others embraced each of us in turn and congratulated us. It was a very happy moment!

"What's wrong with your hand?" Coard asked. I explained to him what had happened. "Please, try... try and control yourself," he said, his voice biting with sarcasm. "We still have 36 police stations to capture; the work has only just begun."

Minutes later another car approached. Redhead and I took up positions at the sentry boxes at the entrance. The car came forward. It stopped.

"Sgt. Bedeau, Royal Grenada Police Force," a voice reported.

From cover Redhead calmly pushed open the gate. As the car came forward slowly, from both sides Redhead and I shouted, "Freeze!" as we pointed our weapons through windows.. We ordered the occupants out and took them prisoners.

And so, the might-have-been captors of the leadership became among the first captives of the Revolution. It was the unit of which Sgt. Bedeau and his companions were a part that had caused the leadership to be left stranded at Freedom Hill and to take hasty refuge in a safe house in that area from where they observed the transformation of the Green Beast barracks into a ball of fire.

What had happened was that after the driver had dropped off Bishop, Coard and Louison at Freedom Hill for their unannounced appearance, and as he proceeded, intending to park the car next to the nearby Calabash Hotel, he observed the presence of security officers in the area. That forced him to make it away quickly, as he dreaded capture. His mind must have been overwhelmed by thoughts of the probable consequences of falling into the hands of the security forces at that moment. He had to get out of there. Thus was the leadership stranded and nearly captured.

Even after the attack at True Blue, the leadership still experienced anxieties before they could get to Radio Grenada. They had obtained a car from the house where they had taken refuge. However, the car was not in good working condition. As they made their way laboriously towards Radio Grenada, Bedeau and his companions were speeding in the direction of True Blue. When they observed the car driven by Bishop, they reversed a bit, as if preparing to give pursuit, but then decided against it. The ball of fire rising above the army camp proved a greater attraction! If they had given immediate pursuit, they certainly would have captured the top leadership of the party.

Not very long after the capture of Bedeau and others, the light of a new day began to make its presence felt, and workers, unaware of the dramatic events unfolding, began arriving to work. Soon Bishop, Coard, Whiteman and Louison had Radio Grenada organised and ready to broadcast.

In True Blue, Gahagan gave instructions to make a thorough search of the compound to ensure that all weapons were collected. While this search was in progress, a fire truck came rushing along intent on putting out the fire. The truck was captured and the occupants taken prisoner. Almost immediately afterwards another detachment led by a Captain in the Green Beast came along. This time the situation ended more seriously. They refused to surrender. They opened fire. Brief fighting ensued. At the end of it, the captain and another security officer lay dead.

The unit, with over 20 prisoners by now, departed True Blue on the march to Radio Grenada shortly thereafter.

After marching one kilometre, another police detachment came rushing along in a green school bus. They encountered the column of NLA members on the True Blue highway. Chalky Ventour led, driving a white car. While the other revolutionary forces took cover on both sides of the road, Ventour immediately turned the car around and reversed it into the oncoming School Bus. The startled bus driver was forced to brake. The car's rear bumped into the front of the bus.

As he told me afterwards, "I quickly put the gear in neutral and allowed the car to hit the bus on its own momentum."

As the vehicles collided, Ventour sprung out from the car, and with pistol drawn he leapt onto the bus, pushing open the door, shouting, "Nobody move! This is the People's Revolution! Put down your guns and come out!" In shock the policemen all dropped their .303 rifles. One by one they came out of the bus with their hands in the air and were all taken prisoners. As life would have it, one of the captured prisoners was Cosmus Richardson who would later join the People's Revolutionary Army (PRA), and end up being one of the Grenada 17 prisoners.

At Radio Grenada, Austin recorded a statement. It was the statement to inform the Grenadian people, and the world of the birth of the Grenada Revolution.

Bishop, Coard, Whiteman and Louison meanwhile eagerly discussed the situation. They were worried that Gahagan had not yet arrived at Radio Grenada with the other forces. Their concern was more than justified, because we were only nine, and we had to control four prisoners. Also, workers, some of whom were sympathetic to Gairy, were in the building. Of much greater concern though was the fact that we were located less than 400 metres away from the Police Training School, which housed about 100 trainees, with weapons available to them.

Finally, the leadership instructed Redhead and me to leave, and contact Gahagan, and ask him to send reinforcements. We left. Five hundred metres away from Radio Grenada, we met a long convoy. At the front, on foot, was a very martial Gahagan, closely followed by Leon Cornwall. Other NLA members lined the sides and back of the convoy. The Revolution was rolling on!

As I informed Gahagan of the preoccupation of the leadership, and of the need to hurry, we heard the words I will never forget: "Attention! Attention! Attention! People of Grenada, the government of the criminal dictator Eric Matthew Gairy has been overthrown." It was the voice of Hudson Austin being relayed over 'Radio Free Grenada, the Voice of the Revolution'. I stood still. Gahagan, Cornwall and other NLA members standing close by all stood still. We looked at each other. In that one moment, in my mind's eye, I relived my entire life. Tears almost in the eyes, we embraced each other. And the convoy rolled on, turning onto the Morne Rouge stretch to go to Radio Free Grenada (RFG).

At the Police Training School, Austin's announcement led to moments of consternation. Then there was a burst of activity. The police officers all grabbed their rifles and prepared to move in and recapture Radio Grenada.

But the NLA unit was also metres away from Radio Grenada. The police on observing the unit took up attacking formation and moved in. Ventour drew his pistol. He pulled the trigger. Click! Click! Click! His pistol was empty. It was only then we realised that he had earlier captured a bus full of policemen with an empty weapon!

Other NLA members were more fortunate and still had ammunition. They unleashed a fusillade forcing the police trainees to retreat in panic.

Minutes after, the unit arrived at Radio Free Grenada. Gahagan quickly proceeded to organise a circular defence. Then I saw Liam Owusu James. He was running in the direction of RFG. His hands were raised in victory. When he saw me, he stopped. The complexion of his face changed;

anger instantaneously replaced elation. He unleashed a stream of imprecations at me. He had waited all night for me to return to lead him to Freedom Hill. All I could do was apologise to him and explain.

Chapter 18

A People's Revolution

"Comrade Prime Minister, you will address the nation at 10.00 a.m.," Coard said, as he scribbled away at a note in his peculiar left-handed style.

"But....but Bernard, we did not discuss who will be Prime Minister."

"I have some points drafted here which we should discuss so that the speech can be properly written up, or else it would not be ready in time," Coard continued, as if he had not heard Bishop. Then he raised his head, and his eyes met Bishop's. "Why are you being so modest, Maurice? You are the leader!" And the air resonated with the loud and happy laughter of Coard rising to his feet, enjoying Bishop's discomfiture.

Bishop kept his seat, his face creased with disbelief; "Is this real?" written all over it. Then he beamed his winsome smile; the smile of a happy bridegroom on his wedding day. No words were needed! The smile said it all.

And so about 7:00 a.m., upstairs Radio Free Grenada, in the manager's office, Maurice Bishop accepted the Prime Ministership of Grenada.

We Move Tonight

From then Bishop and Coard worked together as a team, complementing each other. Bishop, the man of the people, the brilliant orator, the embodiment of charisma; Coard, the brilliant strategist, tactician and organiser, an undoubted genius. Together they worked, with Whiteman, Austin, Louison, Gahagan and Cornwall, spearheading the consummation of the Revolution.

Even before the announcement on the radio by Austin, party militants islandwide were on the move setting up roadblocks, and informing the people of the attack on True Blue. The people, on seeing them do this, at first thought they were going mad. Liam Owusu James once told me that as he moved through St. George on that morning he came across a strong supporter of the Party.

" 'Gairy gone; we overthrow Gairy!' " James said he excitedly told the party supporter. "He just stared at me as though I was mad. The next day a friend in the area told me that the supporter came knocking down his door about 5:00 a.m., after I gave him the news. He seemed shaken, my friend said. 'What happen to Owusu? Like Owusu getting crazy. He just running up and down telling people that Jewel takeover.' "

That kind of shock and disbelief was typical all over Grenada. Even after Austin made the announcement, many people, deeply distrustful of Gairy, still thought that some kind of trick was being played on them. "Gairy ain't catchin' me wit' dhat," was one response. "The bitch just want to see who against him to victimise them," was another response. Despite Austin's call to the people to come down to Radio Free Grenada to collect weapons, only a trickle responded initially.

But in the meantime, the NLA forces, supported by Party activists, displaying white armbands with a red circular dot for identification purposes, efficiently moved on fulfilling their missions. Within two hours of Austin's announcement, three of Gairy's top security officials, including the Acting Commissioner of Police, were captured. Key political officials, including the Deputy Prime Minister, were also captured. Their voices were taped and played on the radio. And when the people heard their voices, conceding defeat and calling on their supporters to surrender, they became convinced. And an explosion of mass activity took place! Thousands of people across the length and breath of Grenada poured onto the streets. They armed themselves with whatever they could lay their hands on, and made off to round up Gairy's henchmen, or help take over police stations. And some also made for RFG.

One very key official was, however, not captured. Senior Attorney-at-Law, Derek Knight Q.C., was one of the top Gairyite leaders. He was the Minister without Portfolio in Gairy's cabinet. It was said in Gairyite circles that he was too intelligent to be confined to any one ministry. For several reasons he was deeply respected and feared by opponents of Gairy; his formidable intellect and reputation for decisiveness, among them. Ironically, Knight was reputed to be the first Marxist in Grenada. And he was the founder of one of Grenada's largest unions – the Technical and Allied Workers' Union (TAWU). When Knight got wind of the move on the True Blue barracks he immediately sought cover. Apparently unaware of the roadblock at the Tanteen roundabout, however, he drove right up to it. The roadblock was controlled by Kamau McBarnette, an NJM leader in the capital, St. George, at the time, later a Central Committee member and Grenada 17 prisoner. Kamau had a decision to make: arrest Derek Knight, or let him through. Something he could not fully explain to himself at the time told him to let Knight through. He did. History proved Kamau's decision correct, although at the time unpopular. Why this turned out to be the correct decision is a tale in itself; beyond the confines of this book.

We Move Tonight

Thus did Knight slip through the revolutionary dragnet and fled the country. He remained abroad for the duration of the Revolution.

About mid-morning on March 13th, I went into the Capital. I went there to obtain medical attention for my injured hand. I was driven there in a small jeep. As we made our way to St. George, traffic flowed in the opposite direction. Janet trucks (so named because they were brought into Grenada after the legendary Hurricane Janet of 1955) loaded with people, were on their way to RFG. These trucks belonged to the Ministry of Works. They were normally used to transport road workers. But on March 13th they were captured by the people. As the trucks passed, the 40-50 persons jammed-in, in the boxing of the truck, would raise their hands in greeting. And cutlasses, forks, spades, stones and the odd rifle could be seen.

To get into St. George we had to go through three roadblocks. At those roadblocks we received further greetings from youths as they stood vigilantly. But one of the most striking things riveted in my mind relates to the police checkpoint in the heart of St. George. The police had evacuated the streets of the town of St. George's, which was fully under control of the revolutionary forces. A public holiday had also been declared by the Revolution to mark the triumph. Workers who had come into town were getting out of St. George. The capital was therefore as busy and as jammed as any peak hour. In the centre of a revolution, with traffic police absent, it was natural to expect chaos in the Capital. But that was not to be. On the traffic point stood a young revolutionary, martially dressed, calmly directing the traffic. I observed that scene for about 20-30 minutes and not once did I see anyone dissent with or challenge his orders to proceed or to stop.

And I also observed that there was no looting of business places in St. George. The same was true for the rest of Grenada. It's significant that in 1974, St. George was looted, by

Gairy's supporters. That was done on Gairy's instigation, as part of his effort to break the general strike. And in 1983, during the American invasion, St. George was again looted. But no such thing took place on March 13th or thereafter.

By the time I arrived back at Radio Free Grenada, the scene there was of quiet efficient organisation. And yet the buzz of excitement and revolutionary purpose was very audible. RFG had been transformed into a genuine Headquarters of the Revolution. People and vehicles lined the streets outside. Young NLA members controlled checkpoints, allowing vehicles to enter and leave. Fifteen additional telephone lines were now installed by Telephone Company workers on their own initiative. They were elated by the uprising. They had immediately begun to monitor calls into and out of Grenada, and calls to key Gairy officials. And indeed, through this monitoring, information leading to the capture of some of Gairy's top people was gathered. In Grenada it normally took months to obtain a telephone line, but the workers, wanting to play their part, provided 15 lines in less than two hours.

With these additional lines, a communications centre was set up. This centre was manned by volunteers, who were continuously on their toes as calls poured in from different parts of Grenada. People called to provide information on the movements of Gairy's supporters, on boats, and on anything they considered suspicious. Countless calls also came in from other Caribbean countries, North America and Europe. I remember one guy who became a kind of legend in the early days of the Revolution while playing a role in running that communications centre. Sometimes he would answer one phone; "Hold on," he would tell the caller, as he raced to answer another phone. "Headquarters of the Revolution. Hold on". And he would race to answer a third phone. And so on. Sometimes he had a phone on each shoulder, one in each hand, and one on a table to attend to. He kept that up for 36 hours straight, until a doctor had to be called in to sedate him.

There was also a small canteen at RFG, which was used to provide meals and refreshments for the small staff which worked at the centre. On March 13th it was transformed into a food supply point. It was stocked up with food of all types and descriptions, which was supplied by the people. There was fresh food, cooked food, vegetables, fruits and what have you. Hundreds of people, if not thousands, were fed at RFG alone on that March 13th, and hundreds more could have been fed.

By evening, the Revolution took on the atmosphere and tempo of a festival, a carnival, rather than an uprising. RFG kept the people lively with calypso music, which was punctuated by Revolutionary Bulletins. These Bulletins were used to direct the Revolution. They provided information on the progress of the Revolution, and directed the revolutionary forces and the masses on what tasks were still to be accomplished to ensure the complete overthrow of Gairy. In all, over 15 Bulletins were issued on March 13th. So decisive were these Bulletins, and the role of the radio station overall, that journalists who followed the progress of the Revolution in the early hours and days dubbed the Grenada Revolution 'Revolution by radio'.

I vividly recall one particular Bulletin: Bulletin No. 10. That bulletin was relayed at about 3:00 p.m. It ended something like this: "Forces of the Revolution, the Mongoose Gang is moving in the direction of West Coast – Deal with them!" When the Mongoose Gang members heard this they panicked. Up until then they were thinking about offering resistance. But when they heard the Bulletin they turned around, and fled in the direction of St. George. They hid in the roof of a school; but they were finally captured. It was a sight to see the vaunted Mongoose Gang come out crawling and begging for mercy. But they were neither harmed nor maltreated. They were taken prisoner and brought to RFG.

By 4:00 p.m., approximately 100 prisoners were being held at RFG. By that time, also, nearly all police stations had surrendered, raising white flags as ordered. As Gairy's henchmen were captured cheers erupted in the villages where they were conquered. There was also cheering along the route to RFG and on entering RFG where they were taken. And as the police stations fell one by one, more and more people took up arms and joined the revolutionary forces.

In a pincer action, forces from St. Andrew spearheaded by Kennedy Budhlall, linked up with forces from St. Patrick, where Tan Bartholomew was the Commander, and forces from St. John, spearheaded by Einstein Louison. These forces swept the entire North and West Coast, marching right into St. George. At the same time forces came down from the St. David and St. Paul's area, sweeping the East and South East Coast. All these forces joined up with forces from St. George to form one massive army of thousands strong. And at the same time, forces remained in all the outer parishes to control the police stations, and other key installations captured, and to establish the dominance of the Revolution.

Just before these forces joined, the final resistance points of the dictatorship fell. Fort George, as it was then, and is now called, capitulated about 4:00 p.m. Fort George was the Headquarters of the police force. The forces there held out for many hours. But they were finally brought to their knees by intense psychological warfare and pressure waged via RFG, and through the surrounding of the Fort.

For hours, 60 armed insurgents surrounded Fort George. These 60 persons were joined by hundreds of other unarmed persons, who called incessantly on the forces in there to surrender amidst warning from RFG via the airwaves that the fort would be attacked if they didn't.

We Move Tonight

In fact, the taking of Fort George had always been a cause of acute concern; that concern went back to the planning days in November 1978. It was felt that a force dug in there, and expecting attack, could only be defeated at the cost of great bloodshed. This, the leadership wanted to avoid; and so they opted for psychological warfare tactics to force the surrender of Police Headquarters.

Right after Police Headquarters fell, a part of the unit which had surrounded there, reinforced by additional men, moved to capture the final stronghold of the old order: Mt. Royal, the home of the dictator himself. A force of about 80 men guarded that location. The majority of the men occupied a barrack immediately outside the gate of the main entrance to Mt. Royal. The rest of the men were based inside Mt. Royal. However, during the day, they had all retreated inside Mt. Royal and occupied the high ground.

Redhead and Chris Stroude led a force of about 50 revolutionaries to capture Mt. Royal. The force was divided into two. One part of the force led by Redhead moved up to Mt. Royal, in the direction of the main entrance. The police inside Mt. Royal concentrated their fire on them. But that was a diversion; the real attack came from the second direction by the other part of the unit led by Stroude. The police were taken by complete surprise. Most dropped their weapons and fled. But quite a number of them were captured and taken prisoner. With Mt. Royal captured, the Revolution was completed. It was a magnificent victory!

In just over 12 hours, the Grenadian masses, led by their vanguard, the NJM, had smashed the Gairy dictatorship. A dictatorship which had ruled Grenada uninterrupted for 12 years; building up a security apparatus of 1390 persons, or thereabout: an army of 200 strong; a 686 man police force; and a voluntary constabulary which included the Mongoose Gang force, of some 470 men.

Throughout that historic Tuesday, March 13th 1979, the world had followed the unfolding events in Grenada with a keen eye. In the Caribbean, the cricket loving people for once forgot cricket, and focused their attention on Grenada. Tony Cozier, commentating on the cricket match, West Indies vs. Australia in the Packer series, matched the scoreboard of the cricket with the scoreboard of the Revolution. He could hold the attention of his listeners in no other way.

In Jamaica, the government of Prime Minister Manley followed events closely. By 9:00 a.m. Prime Minister Bishop was on the phone to Prime Minister Manley. Prime Minister Manley offered immediate recognition to the new government.

Even before then, Prime Minister Bishop had spoken to President Burnham of Guyana. President Burnham immediately recognised the new government; hence his government was the first to recognise the revolutionary government in Grenada. President Burnham also promised to immediately send in military assistance, in the form of arms and training officers. That assistance arrived in Grenada within 24 hours of being promised. Burnham was indeed a great friend who displayed boundless confidence in NJM. Together with Manley, he worked tirelessly and successfully from the first hours to secure international recognition for the Revolution.

In Britain the BBC informed the British people and the world of the dramatic developments in Grenada.

Radio Moscow in the USSR, in its world service broadcast also carried news of the victory of the Revolution.

The China News Agency made the Chinese people aware of the historic developments.

In the United States of America, President Carter assembled the National Security Council. The CIA scrambled to obtain information about Maurice Bishop and the NJM. They were caught totally unawares. Completely naked! Some of their informants suggested that Bishop and the NJM were communist. Others said they were 'wishy-washy socialists'.

Others said they were Trotskyites. And others still said they were simply nationalist.

And in Havana, Cuba – an official of the Communist Party of Cuba (PCC) rushed to inform Selwyn Strachan of the news. He asked Strachan to accompany him. Strachan was taken to a building in downtown Havana. When he entered, he found himself in the imposing presence of Fidel Castro. It was a meteoric rise. In the preceding days he had been unable to see anyone higher than junior functionary level in the Department of the Americas of the PCC.

The Cubans, even in those final days of the Gairy dictatorship, totally disbelieved that NJM was capable of making a revolution. In their disbelief, they had maintained a consistent pattern that they had not upgraded in more than two years. From January 1977 to March 1979, NJM made effort after effort to obtain assistance from the Cuban Revolution to topple Gairy. Bishop and Whiteman had made an open trip to Cuba, with the objective of obtaining assistance. At the time Bishop was Leader of the Opposition. The Head of the Department of the Americas received Bishop and Whiteman. Requests for material assistance were met with smiles and evasions. And Bishop and Whiteman were taken to visit factories, and to observe the workings of the organs of Popular People's Power. Nothing useful came out the trip in the form of material assistance for the NJM or its military wing, the NLA. Coard also made a trip to Cuba. His was a secret trip. He carried maps. He explained the political, social, economic, geographical and military situation in Grenada. And he made requests for material assistance. But he too received nice smiles, many evasions, and a friendly departure with empty hands.

Maybe the Cuban revolutionary leadership was wary of NJM's claims. They were constrained by caution, after being burnt on a number of occasions through assisting organisations and movements in other countries whose words turned out to be more optimistic than the reality permitted. Maybe their caution was justified in that they knew very little about the background, history and experience of NJM. Be that as it may, Strachan's mission was destined to fail, until we Grenadian revolutionaries stunned the Cubans out of their disbelief by making the Grenada Revolution.

Chapter 19

The Story of a Flag

One of the features of March 13th 1979 was the appearance on the streets of Grenada of a flag worn by revolutionary forces, as they moved from target to target. That flag, the red circle against the white background, is now irrevocably associated with the Revolution in the mind of every Grenadian who witnessed the historic events. It has therefore been invested with political content and is now simply referred to as: The Revolution Flag. And yet the design of the flag had nothing to do with any political or ideological message. It was all a matter of convenience.

One of the issues addressed in the planning and preparation stage of the Revolution was that of a method to differentiate friendly forces from enemy. As stated in the text, the thinking of the NJM leadership was that hundreds, even thousands of Grenadians, would rise up and join the revolutionary forces once Gairy's army was routed. Identification of these new forces was therefore important.

I cannot recall all the details, but I know that among Austin, Bishop and Coard it was settled that small flags

121

comprising a red circle against a white background would be used to identify new forces. These flags would be pinned onto the clothing of recruits.

I also recall that the rationale for the design was that nothing could be more conspicuous in day or night than red against a white background. Indeed, I recall someone making the point that this is the reason the Red Cross uses a red cross against a white background. True or not, that was the thinking. What is beyond doubt, however, is that the flag of the Grenada Revolution is identical to the national flag of Japan. This, though, is an accident of history.

I further recall that the cloth and paint for the flags were obtained at a concessionary rate, negotiated by Austin, from a sympathetic businessman. Obviously the businessman was not told the purpose for which the cloth and paint were required. The money to purchase the materials was provided by the NJM NYO. In fact, the party leadership literally commandeered the last $70 in the Youth arm's coffers for this purpose. During the Revolution Cornwall and I would jokingly demand repayment with interest.

The first set of flags was painted by Chris Stroude and my schoolmate who drove Bishop, Coard, Whiteman and Louison on the night of March 12th 1979. These were produced in February 1979. Several hundreds were produced then. However, by March 14th 1979 there must have been several thousand on the streets as people got to work and produced their own.

After March 13th 1979 the flag took on political content. It was used alongside the national flag during the celebration or observation of major events. Indeed, it was suggested by many, with varying degrees of seriousness, that it should replace the independence flag as the national flag.

Chapter 20

The Aftermath

March 13th 1979 marked a high point in the history of Grenada. For four and a half years thereafter, the Grenada Revolution proceeded to indelibly stamp its footprints on the social and political landscape of Grenada, and indeed the Caribbean. This it did until tragedy befell the Revolution. That tragedy was preceded by a split in the revolutionary movement as many of the persons referred to in this story lined up against each other. That tragedy resulted in the deaths of Maurice Bishop and Unison Whiteman, among others. It occasioned the invasion of Grenada by the mighty United States, and the final smashing of the Revolution. It also resulted in the imprisonment of Bernard Coard, Hudson Austin, Selwyn Strachan, Liam Owusu James, Leon Cornwall, Chris Stroude, Lester Redhead, Dave Tan Bartholomew and myself; all convicted for the deaths of Bishop and Whiteman. We would spend a longer period on death row than the life of the Revolution.

These events have raised many issues including those of revolutionary legality and substantive justice versus procedural justice; but such issues are beyond this book.

However, having told the story of how the Grenada Revolution was made, I consider it fit and proper to address the issue of the genesis of the revolution, the broader context in which the events unfolded and the influences which shaped the personalities who spearheaded the revolutionary process. Part B deals with these topics.

Photographs

*

Maurice Bishop, PM of Grenada 1979-1983

Joseph Ewart Layne

Bernard Coard, Deputy PM of Grenada 1979-1983

From left, Chester Humphrey, Bernard Coard, and Jim
Wardally 1979

We Move Tonight

Lester Redhead

Maurice Bishop right, and St. George's businessman, Chasley David

Joseph Ewart Layne

John Chalky Ventour

Vincent Noel

Kenrick Radix   George Louison

Kenrick Radix right, with PM Maurice Bishop

131

Leon Bogo Cornwall

Basil Aki Gahagan

Unison Whiteman

Joseph Ewart Layne

The author left, Tan Bartholomew right, and others

Selwyn Strachan addressing road workers, Queens Park, 1980

134

Dr. David Lambert as a young soldier

Kennedy Bhudlall

Eric Gairy, Leader of Grenada, 1951-57, 1961-62, 1967-79

Sir Eric Gairy, Prime Minister of Grenada, 1974-79

Hudson Austin centre, Basil Gahagan far right and Cubans

From left Liam James, Hudson Austin, Desi Bouterse of
Surinam, and Maurice Bishop

PM Maurice Bishop, with Daniel Ortega of Nicaragua

On podium, Daniel Ortega, Maurice Bishop, with Michael
Manley of Jamaica, taking a salute in Grenada 1980

Einstein Louison, fifth from left, Vistrel Military Academy USSR, 1983

The author, fifth from left, Vistrel Military Academy USSR, 1983

*

PART B

The Broader Context

*

Chapter 21

Birth of NJM

The New Jewel Movement (NJM) was formed on March 11th 1973, in St. David. It emerged from the unity of two revolutionary organisations: Movement for Assemblies of the People (MAP) and Joint Endeavour for the Welfare, Education and Liberation of the people (JEWEL).

Maurice Bishop, a young Grenadian British-trained lawyer who returned to Grenada in 1970, was the founder and leader of MAP. MAP originated in the capital parish of St. George. It was formed in September 1972. Its main area of work was revolutionary education among its members and among the youths around Grenada. By March 11th 1973, MAP had direct links with thirty-six groups of youths loosely organised around the country. It is, I believe, true to say that these groups had an organisational link with MAP, though, as I understand it, that relationship cannot be put higher than one of loose affiliation.

Unison Whiteman, a Grenadian teacher who studied Economics and Political Science at Howard University in the USA, was the founder and leader of JEWEL, which originated in St. David. JEWEL was formed in the period February – March 1972.

In addition to being leader of JEWEL, Whiteman was also a member of MAP. And so he became the main agent and link in the subsequent merger of the two organisations into NJM. JEWEL's main area of work was the publication of a weekly newspaper named JEWEL, and the operation of a co-operative farm based in St. David. The paper pursued a militant editorial policy and served to awaken the consciousness of the Grenadian populace to the ills of the decadent Gairy regime, and to galvanise the masses into action against Gairyism.

Selwyn Strachan, was another of the links between MAP and JEWEL, being active in both organisations.

I believe that it would be correct to say that JEWEL was the more militant and active of the two organisations. However, both organisations co-operated in their activities. And in Maurice Bishop, MAP possessed the young leader with the greatest popular appeal in the country.

The first time I can remember taking cognisance of Bishop was in the now famous Nurses Demonstration in 1970. A number of nurses at the General Hospital, the main hospital in Grenada, went on strike to protest against the deplorable conditions existing at the hospital at the time. The progressive movement, then in its nascent stage, rallied to the side of the nurses. In November 1970, led by young progressives and supported by a number of youths, the nurses staged a demonstration in downtown St. George. I happened to be in the capital that day. My mother had taken me to visit the doctor to obtain treatment for nasal and respiratory problems, which have plagued me since childhood. When we arrived there a number of people were already waiting to visit the doctor. My mom, then a worker in a commercial business, could not wait. She made the arrangement for me to see the doctor and left, promising to return at 4:00 p.m. to meet me.

No sooner had she left than I saw a crowd moving in the direction of the Health Centre. Health problems and doctor appointment forgotten, I raced in the direction of the

We Move Tonight

Health Centre. There, for the first time, I heard Bishop speak. He was addressing the crowd. He praised the nurses for their patriotism, selflessness and courage in defying Gairy, and on their taking a stand on behalf of poor Grenadians whose only access to medical care was at the General Hospital. His stately manner as he stood, dressed in his court attire, the melodious cadence of his voice, and the enthusiastic response he received as he addressed the crowd, are indelibly printed on my mind.

Another unforgettable memory imprinted on my mind was Gairy's response to that activity: police were sent in to break up the demonstration, with the use of tear gas. I can remember people in the crowd shouting, "Wet your handkerchiefs and bar you eyes and nose," as tear gas fumes enveloped the area. For me it was my baptism in revolutionary activity; a baptism I will never forget.

I will also never forget the anxiety and anger of my mother when she finally caught up with me. With a glib tongue and feigned regret , I tried to talk her anger away, but to no avail. On our arrival home I earned a 'good cut-arse' to round off an eventful day.

Before 1973, I also knew Unison Whiteman well. I had ample opportunity to observe him from close up, for he taught me history at the Presentation Brother's College (PBC). He was a very quiet but amiable man, who exuded a deep personal commitment to the cause of the Grenadian working people.

At the Founding Congress of the New Jewel Movement, Bishop and Whiteman were elected joint co-ordinating secretaries, thereby formally sharing the leadership. A twelve member executive — Political Bureau[20] also emerged. The Political Bureau's task was to give day-to-day political guidance to the work of the NJM.

Bureau members included:
Bernard Coard
George Brizan
Kenrick Radix

Joseph Ewart Layne

Teddy Victor
Sebastian Thomas

Shortly after the Founding Congress, Selwyn Strachan, Jacqueline Creft and Lloyd Noel became members of the Bureau.

Coard, then a University lecturer based in Trinidad, was trained in Economics and Political Science at Brandeis University in the USA, and Sussex University in Britain. He maintained links in Grenada by returning home on a regular basis to participate in the activities of MAP.

Kenrick Radix, was another young Grenadian British trained lawyer, who became a Minister in the PRG during the Revolution.

George Brizan, an educator, trained in Economics and Education at Carleton University and Calgary in Canada, dropped out of the NJM organisational structure at an early stage. However he continued to live in Grenada and served the country as an outstanding educator and economist. After the demise of the revolution he re-entered politics. He was a member of the first post-invasion parliament and was prime minister for short period in 1995.

Teddy Victor, a farmer and small businessman, was one of the founders of JEWEL. He was extremely active in the 1973-1974 period. He was a leading member of the NLA in that period. However, he dropped out of the movement after the 1973-74 defeat. He was detained during the Revolution for "counter revolutionary activities".

Sebastian Thomas, popularly known as 'Sambas', was, another small businessman. He was one of the live wires of JEWEL and of the early NJM.

Selwyn Strachan was from the fishing village of Woburn, which was represented by Eric Gairy in parliament. He would eventually become one of the top organisers of the party and a top leader of the Revolution.

Lloyd Noel, was another young brilliant Grenadian British trained lawyer.. At the Duffus Commission of Inquiry into political disturbances in Grenada in 1973-74, he along with Bishop and Radix formed a powerful team of NJM attorneys. Their outstanding performance before the commission helped to further raise the profile of the young political movement.

Jacqueline Creft was one of the leading female activists in Grenada. She received her academic training in Canada, obtaining a degree in Sociology from Carleton University. She was the Minister of Education and Culture during the years of the Grenada Revolution. She was tragically killed on October 19th 1983.

Another of the founders of NJM was Keith Mitchell, Grenada's current (2013) prime minister. Mitchell received his early university training at the University of the West Indies (UWI), Cave Hill Campus, Barbados. He would subsequently obtain a PHD in mathematics from the American University in Washington. He would emerge to be the leading politician in post 1983 Grenada, being prime minister from 1995-2008. He once again became prime minister in February 2013.

Chapter 22

The 1951 Revolution[21]
And its Consequences

The birth of NJM came at the end of a period of economic, sociological and constitutional/political change in Grenada.[22] It also came during a period when a wind of political change was blowing through the Caribbean.

Up until 1951, agriculture was the dominant and prospering sector of Grenada's economy – prospering, that is, for the planter class of Grenada and the British colonial system. But in 1951, the agricultural workers rose up against the planter class and British Colonial control.[23] For 100 years since the emancipation from slavery, in 1838, the wages of generations of agricultural workers remained relatively unchanged. After 1940 small wage increases were granted.[24] But it was too little too late. By 1951 labour oppression combined with(i) the aspirations for improvement among agricultural workers on the estates, (ii) the hope for improvement aroused by the small wage increases of the previous decade and (iii) further inspired by the labour struggles in other Caribbean islands all served to form a powder keg in Grenada waiting for ignition.[25]

We Move Tonight

In 1950, a 29-year-old Grenadian who had been active in the Labour Movement in the oil-belt of the Dutch Antilles returned to Grenada. His name was Eric Gairy. He met a situation waiting for leadership, and offering the possibility for satisfying his ambition to obtain a political mass base and political power.

Gairy formed a labour union, the Grenada Manual and Mental Workers Union (G.M.M.W.U.), into which he unionised Grenada's 10,000 agricultural workers, spread on many estates all around Grenada. He began to champion their cause for higher wages and better working conditions and to challenge the planter class. At first, he was branded a communist and was ignored by the planters; but he kept up the struggle. Finally, in 1951, the situation erupted. The keg exploded! Widespread protest broke out on the estates![26]

During what has become known as the 1951 "Revolution", agricultural workers burned and destroyed estates, and installations – schools, medical centres, the Governor's Beach House – symbols of the colonial dominance in the island. Anger, pent up over 100 years, against ruthless economic exploitation, deprivation of political power and colonial oppression burst its dam.[27]

The British responded in the usual manner. Military and para-military forces were brought in from Barbados, St. Vincent and neighbouring islands in an effort to quell the uprising. But they met with little success. Gairy was arrested and taken on a British warship. This, too, failed to quell the uprising.[28]

Recognising that rather than serving to arrest the situation, the use of force fuelled the uprising, the British finally played the compromise card. They extended the carrot. In an astute assessment, borne out by subsequent events , a leading British Official who came to Grenada and met with Gairy, assessed him as a demagogue and an egotist, whose main interest was personal power, and who was capable of being bought and manipulated.[29] He proposed that a compromise be struck with Gairy. This compromise finally brought an end to the uprising.

Out of that 1951 struggle, agricultural workers won substantial improvements in their daily wages, and working conditions. Also, very importantly, they won for themselves a sense of dignity and respect as they forced the planters and British to back down for the first time ever! The 1951 experience proved that Rights could be won through struggle.[30]

The social changes spawned by the 1951 events were so wide ranging and impactful that many have referred to that period as the 1951 Revolution. This author fully endorses this description.

After the 1951 struggle, the Grenadian populace first exercised the right to vote as universal adult suffrage was instituted.[31] The colonialists, however, reserved for themselves the power to nominate members to the Parliament; and they maintained control over the country's finances.[32]

The 1951 "Revolution" also marked the beginning of a rapid decline of agriculture in Grenada. With the decline of agriculture came the decline of the planter class. Many of the planters, shaken by the explosion, sold out and fled the country; others simply abandoned their estates. This decline was accelerated by Hurricane Janet which swept Grenada on September 22nd 1955, wreaking havoc on the agricultural sector. In an effort to stave off decline, members of the planter class shifted some of their investments from agriculture to the emerging commercial and manufacturing sectors.[33] The post 1951 period was also a time of migration of the educated working class to the Metropolis.

In 1967 there were elections under the new constitutional system providing full internal self-government. Gairy and his GULP rose to real power for the first time. He used that power to virtually complete the demise of the agriculture power base of the old ruling class planter elements. Gairy confiscated most of their estates; some of these estates he transformed into state farms; and others were distributed to his supporters in what he called a 'Land for the Landless Programme'.[34] Between 1967 and 1973, Gairy, through executive action, also seized control of two of the three agricultural produce co-operatives existing on the island, namely: the Grenada Cocoa Industry Board; and the Banana Co-operative Society. These two co-operatives unified all the country's farmers involved in the production of those two crops. They controlled millions of dollars in cash and other resources but functioned independently of the government. These boards were mainly under the control of the big planters. Their seizure, therefore, represented a major blow against their power and influence. And finally in 1975–1976, after an extremely fierce struggle with the planters who were allied with the upper and middle peasantry, Gairy also seized control of the Grenada Co-opeative Nutmeg Association (GCNA) thereby completing a clean sweep of the agricultural sector of the economy, and the economic base of the planter class. The GCNA was by far the richest of the three co-operatives, having millions of dollars in the bank; it had over 7,000 members, though it was under the firm control of the big planters and upper peasantry.

Thus, through his own authoritarianism, Gairy sowed the seeds of dissent, since a large number of middle and small farmers, and former estate workers, shared a stake in the protective cooperatives and felt threatened by the loss of autonomy which these cooperatives provided. Parallel feelings of dissent, and grievances, linked to deteriorating economic circumstances caused by the decline of agriculture, arose both in urban and rural areas among small farmers, teachers, policemen, new landowners, and disenfranchised former estate workers.

Chapter 23

The Rise of the Dictator

With the attainment of adult suffrage, party politics was introduced to Grenada. In 1951 Gairy formed his Grenada United Labour Party (GULP). The other major party to emerge in Grenada before NJM was the Grenada National Party (GNP). This was the party born of an alliance of the declining planter class, the urban merchant class, and elements of the then existing (small) urban professional middle strata. The GNP was formed in 1955. [35]

Members of the aspiring and still nascent black middle-class took up the leading positions within GULP. The 10,000 agricultural workers, on whose behalf Gairy had struggled during the 1951 Revolution, though, provided the political mass base of the party.

In the 1951 general elections, the first held in Grenada under conditions of adult suffrage, GULP won the majority of the seats in the Parliament. Gairy thus emerged as the first black man to be leader of Grenada, where about 90% of its population was and still remains black. And this commenced the rise of Eric Gairy to political ascendancy and dominance in Grenada.[36]

154

After his victory in 1951, Gairy won the 1954 elections. He lost the 1957 elections, although he won 49% of the vote. (The island's population was then approximately 60,000). But he was returned to office after his party won the 1961 elections. He himself did not participate in that general election; he was then disenfranchised. The disenfranchisement by the British was imposed on him for allegedly invading a political meeting of the opposing party with a group of his supporters and breaking it up. However, shortly after his party secured victory at the elections, one of its parliamentarians resigned his seat to allow Gairy to participate in a bye-election. He won that bye-election and assumed his position as head of government. [37]

By then a constitutional change provided the new Gairy government with control of the country's finances. And Gairy himself took on the post of Minister of Finance, in addition to being Chief Minister.

No sooner had Gairy gained control of the country's finances, than he and his cohorts began a pattern of misuse of public finances and corruption. But they were cut down in their strides. The British government, still maintaining overall and effective control of the country and benefiting handsomely from the trade imbalances, moved in. In late 1961-early 1962, the British government suspended the constitution and ousted Gairy from political office. This action followed the submission of the report of a Commission of Inquiry, which had investigated the spending of public funds in Grenada in 1961. The Commission found much evidence of widespread corruption and misuse of public funds. The Commission held Eric Gairy responsible for much of it. That scandal has since been recorded in Grenada's political folklore as "Squandermania".[38]

Subsequent to Squandermania – in 1962 – elections were called. Gairy's party lost the elections to the GNP. Five years later though, capitalising on the complete incompetence and anti-worker policies of the GNP government, Gairy's party was returned to power. That GNP government was led by Herbert Blaize. By that time (1967) Grenada had become an Associated State with Britain, a status that had brought internal self-government to Grenada. Gairy therefore came to office, to wield effective control of the entire state machinery.[39]

After the 1967 elections, the black aspiring petit-bourgeoisie, increasingly growing into a merchant class, finally supplanted the old planter class elements as the dominant stratum within the Grenadian ruling class. This stratum, eager to enjoy the spoils long denied them, quickly returned to "Squandermania" habits, enjoying the fruits of corruption. They fleeced the Grenadian masses, utilising resources of the state to enrich themselves. They sold out public property to each other at a pittance, used public materials and resources to carry out private construction, and they utilised the state power they now controlled to enrich their business allies. This they did by dishing out monopoly and oligopoly rights to themselves, in key commodities. Sugar and rice importation were two cases of vital necessities placed by Gairy under the monopoly/oligopoly control of his close black business (and political) allies within this newly emerged control group. This activity by Gairy and his allies heightened the contradiction with the old ruling class elements as the latter were further squeezed out of areas of economic activity. The commodities placed under their monopoly/oligopoly control were then resold at exorbitant profits, robbing the Grenadian masses of millions of dollars, and driving the price of basic products sky-high while real wages fell.[40]

Gairy's dramatic personal enrichment epitomises the extravagance with which this class robbed the Grenadian populace. In the period before the 1967 elections 17 debt cases were brought against Gairy by individuals and firms seeking to recover money owed to them. Three of those cases arose out of debts incurred as late as 1965. Those three debts totalled just over $1,000 ($1,050). But Gairy was in such dire economic straits, that he could not repay any of his debts.[41] Indeed, by 1967 he was on the verge of being declared a bankrupt when the election emerged to save the day. Yet by 1973, Gairy on a monthly salary of about $5,000 had become a millionaire with interest in many businesses. (He was also reputed to have large sums of cash stashed away in Swiss bank accounts.) By 1979 his total property in Grenada alone was valued at $25m (EC).[42]

To entrench his dominance over the state machinery, Gairy pursued a policy of naked victimisation. In the bureaucracy, the police, prison service, education structures and health system, he fired left, right and centre people who opposed him; and replaced them with his supporters. And for additional muscle, he institutionalised and gave free reign to his Ton Ton Macoutes referred to by Grenadians as the Mongoose Gang.[43]

Chapter 24

Social and Political Changes and the Development of NJM Leadership

The decline of agriculture that started in 1951 also led to the movement of population from rural to urban areas. This was an important sociological development with great political significance. Out of this movement of population came the expansion of the urban working class in numbers and importance. The development of the transitional strata of unemployed, semi-employed and part-time artisans also emerged out of that change.[44] These strata were added to, as succeeding generations came to adulthood, and as the economy of the urban centres proved increasingly unable to provide jobs for its swelling numbers; commerce, manufacturing and tourism could not fill in totally for the declining agricultural sector. The end result of this was the development of unemployment, which reached over 30% by 1973.

With the expansion of educational opportunities in the post World War II Caribbean and in Grenada, more sons and daughters of poor and black Grenadians were able to obtain secondary school education[45]. Some of these young Grenadians were also able to leave Grenada to pursue higher education in North America and Britain, where conditions were improving for the working classes generally.

It was some of the Grenadians who went to Britain and North America, in the early and mid-1960's, who returned to Grenada at the end of the '60's and early '70's to become the founders and leaders of NJM.

In North America and Britain they had experienced the effects of racism and witnessed the changes and turbulence in those countries. These young and budding leaders witnessed first-hand and followed closely: the rise and astounding successes of the civil rights movement in the US under the leadership of Martin Luther King Jr.; the rise and activity of the Black Power movement as a whole, and of individuals like Malcolm X, Stokely Carmichael and Rap Brown; massive demonstrations in the US and Britain and all over Europe, in the wake of the famous Tet Offensive in the Vietnam War which forced the US to start pulling out its forces from Vietnam shortly after; student unrest in Europe and North America; the assassinations of Martin Luther King Jr. and Malcolm X, and the wave of protests which followed; the escalation in activity of the national liberation movements in Asia, Africa and Latin America; the formation of the Non-aligned Movement, following on from the Bandung conference in 1955 of Asian and African states, and its flourishing in the '70's. And more! All these experiences were to have lasting effects on those young Grenadians. They deepened their love and ambition for their country, and their willingness to return to their homeland to save it, by struggling to improve it.

By the time the soon-to-be revolutionary leaders arrived back home, the wind of change which they had experienced in the metropolis had reached the Caribbean. In 1968 it swept through Jamaica when what has become known as the (Walter) Rodney Riots erupted. And by 1970 it was right next door. In Trinidad and Tobago – Revolution was sweeping that land.

The Grenada to which these young leaders returned at the end of the '60's and early 70's was of a different social and political order to the one in which Gairy came to political prominence in 1951.

The agricultural workers on whose behalf Gairy fought in 1951 remained at the bottom of the social ladder, despite Gairy's being in power. But they continued to fervently support Gairy, being ever thankful to him. They had also greatly declined in numbers. From 10,000 in 1951, they were between 2,000 and 3,000 in 1970 and under 2,000 in 1979.[46] This decline mirrored the decline of agriculture on the whole, and the estate economy in particular. It also mirrored the steady downward trend in Gairy's mass base over the period after 1951, and the decline in his hard-core mass base forged on the 1951 battlefields.

The urban working class, many of whom were sons and daughters and grandchildren of agricultural workers, now opposed Gairy. They were very young or were unborn in 1951 when Gairy struggled on behalf of their forebears. They grew up experiencing the increasing hardship of life in a changing Grenada, and seeing with their own eyes the corruption of Gairyism. The transitional strata, and the youth masses in general, were opposed to Gairy. Besides the economic hardships which produced many unemployed, they were also swept along by the black consciousness movement which by then was having earth-shattering impact in the Caribbean. And in the vast majority of cases, they were the victims of rising police brutality. Middle strata workers in the bureaucracy, schools and health system were also opposed to Gairy. They experienced the disruption and disintegration of their structures as wholesale victimisation was carried out, and corruption spread from the top, through the veins of their organisations. The peasantry, greatly disaffected by the seizure of the agricultural produce co-operatives, and also affected by the overall decline in agriculture, were also opposed to Gairy. They were about 8,000 in all, and thus they formed a very important class in the society. And the old ruling class elements were extremely bitter and disaffected as they saw the erosion of their economic means and influence, which was the objective and natural consequence of Gairy's action against them.[47]

And so with major sections of the population disaffected, Grenadians demanded change. Simmering unrest existed in the country. This simmering unrest was best evidenced by the aforesaid Nurses Demonstrations in November 1970.

Gairy's response to this unrest was to unleash terror to crush it before it exploded. For this task he strengthened the repressive arm of the state. In a notorious speech in 1970, now recorded in Grenada's political folklore as the Black Power Speech, Gairy read the riot act! Alluding to the uprising then taking place in Trinidad and the simmering unrest in Grenada he said, "When your neighbour's house is on fire wet yours," and he went on to describe the water he was going to wet Grenada with. He said,

> *I have recruited the toughest and roughest roughnecks in the land...I will meet steel with steel...I will nip it [unrest] in the bud.*[48]

After that speech, he organised the Night Ambush Squad, the Volunteers for the Protection of Private Property, and he expanded the role of the Mongoose Gang. These forces were unleashed on the population.

And while all these events were unfolding, over 60% of the population of Grenada in 1970 like me was unborn or still children: (63.5% of Grenada's population in 1970 was under 25 years of age). And so I learned of the winds of change from my parents or from books. But from the Nurses Demonstration through the Black Power Speech onwards, I cannot forget, for the events that subsequently unfolded shook Grenada and changed my life forever. Despite Gairy's boast and firm resolve, he was unable to nip the unrest in the bud. It escalated. And with it brutalisation also escalated. Youths were beaten and brutalised in all parishes of Grenada as they protested in several forms ranging from the mode of dress to the style of walk, to demonstrations. And students, who also protested, were regularly beaten as they returned to their homes at nights from studies.[49] These beatings, however, simply spawned more protest.

In 1972 general elections were once more held. Gairy, utilising his control over the electoral machinery, which he enjoyed for the first time – as a result of internal self-government – rigged the elections and awarded himself 13 of 15 parliamentary seats.[50] After the elections Gairy embarked on a process to take Grenada into complete political independence from Britain. This became a major issue in Grenada, as there was great apprehension and indeed downright fear in many quarters about what life would be in a Grenada under the absolute control of Eric Gairy.

Chapter 25

The 1973–1974 Revolution

By March 1973 when NJM was born, open protest had broken out among broad sections of the people who wanted Gairy out. The newly formed NJM, championing the cause of the ordinary working people in Grenada, demanded change. It demanded that Grenada obtain not Flag Independence, but genuine independence, a pre-requisite of which was the removal from power of the corrupt ruler, who had grown into a dictator; and the transfer of power to the people.[51] The old ruling class elements were also fearful of Grenada going into independence under Gairy. They dreaded the removal of the British eye on a Grenada under Gairy. To them anything, even continued colonial rule, was better than Gairy. They were prepared to support any action to get him out. They too, therefore, increasingly joined the masses in open protest against Gairy.

Within weeks of its formation, NJM established itself firmly as the most vibrant and leading political force in Grenada in opposition to Gairy. It led the people in a mass protest action against Gairy. The action was sparked off when

Jeremiah Richardson, a youth from St. Andrew, was shot dead by Gairy's police on April 20th 1973. Within hours NJM leaders were on the spot in St. Andrew. Thousands threw in their support in protest in the next three days. They marched to Pearl's Airport, then the only airport in Grenada, where Jeremiah Richardson had been a worker, and shut it down. That shut-down which lasted for two days was the incident which first brought the Grenadian struggle into regional and international spotlight, as no aircraft could either arrive or leave Grenada. Gairy sent in his forces to quell the disturbance. But NJM had firmly arrived on the Grenadian political landscape. The struggle continued and heightened after that, straining every tissue of Grenada's body politic.

The tension was reflected in my very home, creating strains in our family unit. My father, who by that time was a senior officer in the police force, had given over 30 years' service. He was the only son of an agricultural worker, and grew up in the typical poor Grenadian home of the 1930's and '40's. By 1951 he was already a man of 29 years old, and even though he was a member of the police force he could not but welcome the change brought by the 1951 Revolution. Those changes were reflected close to him, in the improved life of his mother and other immediate relatives.

Understandably, therefore, he supported Gairy. We though – his children by his wife (our mother) – were all born after 1951. We all attended secondary schools – an opportunity our father never had. We came to know Gairy through reports and evidence of his notoriety. And young as we were, we were activated by the unrest in the country; and we opposed Gairy. My friends and my brothers' friends got beaten up regularly, as we participated in protests in the streets against these actions. One of my elder brothers was very active in student affairs, rising to be leader of the Presentation College Students' Council in the 1972–1973 school year. He played an active role in organising protests against Gairy. But at the same time, my father was still a member of the police force. We all still loved him as a father, but something was not right; there were strains. The conflict arising out of the situation weighed on him and he took to drinking, even though according to my mom he never took a drink until he was well past thirty; and even after that he was no more than a social drinker. His heart finally broke in 1973.

One evening he was returning from work, when, under the influence of alcohol he lost control and his car ran off the road. Miraculously he escaped unhurt. But when two of his children (my elder twin brothers) and some friends were going to recover the car, they were not so lucky. They were stopped by Gairy's thugs and arrested. Gairy's thugs proceeded to terrorise my brothers, shaving their heads, throwing them into cells and placing them on trumped-up charges of being in possession of marijuana.

Days later, my father, a broken man, went on leave, and then retired from the police. This story, in different forms, played out in countless homes across the island; it could be related by thousands of youths, whose grandparents, and parents, came from poor background and thus benefited from the 1951 Revolution. It mirrored the changes, the divisions, and strains in Grenada in 1973. It is a story of the Grenada in which NJM was born.

The NJM, from very early, outlined its policies in the now famous NJM Manifesto. The manifesto was written in the months of July and August 1973. The main authors of the manifesto were Maurice Bishop and Bernard Coard. George Brizan also made a contribution to the elaboration of the manifesto. In its political aspect, the manifesto advocated the establishment of people's power through grass root democracy in the form of assemblies of the people, to be based in all the villages of Grenada. And in its economic aspect, it advocated national development along non-capitalist lines.[52]

In November 1973, the young NJM produced its first major challenge for power to the Gairy dictatorship. On 4th

November NJM held its historic People's Congress. Over 10,000 Grenadians, or about 20% of the adult population, turned out to the Congress. There, NJM leaders presented the NJM Manifesto to the Grenadian people. The Manifesto was adopted by the People's Congress as the Programme for bringing genuine independence to Grenada. A People's Indictment was also presented against the dictator.

The indictment contained 27 counts, ranging from murder to embezzlement of public funds. Bishop and Coard, combining their legal and political science skills drafted the indictment. The Congress found Gairy guilty on all 27 counts as charged; he was given two weeks – 14 days – to give up the reins of power. A 54-man caretaker government was elected to take over in the period before popular elections were held. The People's Congress also decided that if Gairy failed to comply with the verdict and will of the people, then a general strike would be called with the objective of ousting him from power.

Gairy responded to this challenge with violence. On 18th November, the deadline for Gairy's resignation, six leaders of the NJM were attacked by Gairy's thugs and were battered. They were in St. Andrew located on the East Coast of Grenada. They were there to finalise the general strike mandated by the People's Congress. That day is now recorded in Grenada's history as Bloody Sunday. Those most severely brutalised on that day were Maurice Bishop, Unison Whiteman and Selwyn Strachan. After being battered, they were thrown in a cell. Cellmates included Hudson Austin, Kenrick Radix and Simon Daniel.

The next day, in their battered state, the NJM Six were taken before a magistrate. The magistrate promptly packed them off to prison, denying them bail to which they were entitled given the nature of the charges against them. Bishop, Whiteman and Strachan, in particular, received no medical care for their manifest injuries.[53]

Far from controlling the restiveness in the country, the brutalisation of the NJM Six exacerbated the situation. In a show of national unity, urban workers, farmers, businessmen, students and the churches protested against the brutality meted out. Workers spontaneously took strike action; students refused to go to school; dockworkers closed down the only port in Grenada; and anti-Gairy demonstrations broke out. Gairy had clearly overplayed his hand!

The brutalisation of the NJM Six also raised to prominence another question: How was the growing revolutionary movement to respond to the use of force by Gairy to crush the revolutionary tide? The formation of the NLA was the answer to this question.

During the '73-'74 revolutionary upsurge, the NLA undertook several actions against the dictatorship. Weapons and explosives were seized from Gairy's forces, and some targets were attacked. However, like the NJM itself, the NLA lacked the organisational capacity and maturity to topple Gairy.

However, it was becoming clear to some, even then, that the government could not be changed through the ballot, as long as Gairy controlled the voting machinery. Those were not yet the days of international observer teams to supervise elections!

Chapter 26

Learning From Defeat:
Charting A New Course

The failure of the '73-'74 revolutionary upsurge was an extremely hard blow for the young progressive and revolutionary movement. At the height of the demonstrations, 25,000 Grenadians were in the streets. These mass protests took place on a daily basis – except Sundays – for a full three weeks. Gairy violently crushed the demonstrations. He sent in his forces to attack a crowd of close to 25,000. In the process, Rupert Bishop, the father of Maurice Bishop, was murdered. This, however, did not break the back of the crippling general strike, which was in progress. For over two months Grenada was cut off from the outside world, and the economy was shut down. And in the midst of the mass demonstrations and general strike, the NLA launched its isolated attacks. But Gairy survived all this. And finally, the revolutionary upsurge subsided. The Revolution failed!

This defeat led to widespread disillusionment, even cynicism, and much soul-searching. Many persons who were active in the revolutionary upsurge left the country, to pursue academic studies overseas, or to take up residence. Others simply dropped out of the struggle.

In the immediate aftermath of the defeat, the task was no longer that of taking on Gairy, but picking up the pieces and rebuilding the movement for the next round. This rebuilding work began from a pretty solid base. For despite the defeat, some very important gains accrued to the revolutionary movement as a result of the upsurge. For one thing, the NJM with its brand of popular politics emerged as the alternative to Gairyism, in the process supplanting the Grenada National Party (GNP) as the leading opposition force to Gairy in the country. And secondly, in Maurice Bishop, the Grenadian masses had recognised a young leader capable of replacing Gairy at the helm of the country.

Bernard Coard played the leading role in the post-mortem analyses and in charting the road for rebuilding the NJM. Coard wrote a number of papers analysing the upsurge and subsequent defeat, and proposing a way forward. These papers he presented to the party leadership and strong supporters of the party.

Let me recall one such presentation. It took place at the Grenada Boys Secondary School (GBSS) in December 1974. It was the first occasion that I met Coard in person. The paper presented by Coard that night at the GBSS was subsequently published. It became a kind of programme for rebuilding the party.

The hub of Coard's analysis was that the NJM was unable to consummate the '73-'74 Revolution, because the party lacked the organisational capacity necessary to do so. He said that the party's internal structure was too loose and amorphous, and that the looseness of the internal structure was reflected in the party's loose links with the masses.

In this regard, Coard pointed out that although the party enjoyed the support and sympathy of a sizeable percentage of the population, no organised day-to-day links existed with these sections. The lack of those links, Coard argued, contributed decisively to the defeat. To concretise the point, Coard said that the party brought out 25,000 people in the streets to protest, but after Gairy crushed the demonstrations, the party lost control and command of the struggle; no structures existed to reach out to the people and influence them while they were off the streets; and hence when the right-wing trade union leaders decided to call off the general strike, at the moment when Gairy was at the point of breaking, the party could do nothing about it: no structures, no organised relationship existed with the working people to influence them to struggle on.

Coard said that to correct the problem, the party had to re-organise itself internally, to enable it to build organised links with the Grenadian masses. He said that the NJM had to be transformed from a 'crowd politics party' to a party with day-to-day links with the masses, without losing its mass appeal; from a party of spontaneous activity, active only when the occasion to bring out the crowd arose, to a party of organised day-to-day activity; from a loose amorphous party, to a vanguard party.

Elsewhere, Coard concretised his ideas on how the NJM should be reorganised and rebuilt. One plank of his plan required the establishment of new criteria for membership in the party. Whereas before, membership was dependent upon purchasing a membership card, the re-organisation programme required party members to be organised in work committees of the party, and to carry out work on behalf of the party on a regular and consistent basis.

Another plank of the plan required the development of a support structure in the villages. Party members and strong supporters of the party were now to be required to organise party groups in their communities. These groups would be expected to meet on a fortnightly or monthly basis. They were to undertake tasks on behalf of the party such as fund raising and distribution of the party newspaper, among others.

170

A third plank of the reorganisation programme required the party to develop links with the people in their – the people's own – organisations. In other words, for the party to develop links within the trade union movement, youth movement, women's movement, farmer's movement, student movement, and professional organisations. Party members belonging to these organisations were to see it as a responsibility to work to win sympathisers within these organisations for the party and its cause. This work, though, was to be carried out without compromising the independence of those organisations, or disrupting their unity.

This programme for rebuilding the party for the next round of the struggle was gradually implemented over a two-year period. It was the results of this programme in its post-nascent stage which enabled the NJM, working in the context of the People's Alliance, to undertake the 1976 general elections campaign; an election in which the People's Alliance won six of 15 seats in Parliament, and 87% of the youth vote. As a result, Maurice Bishop became the official Leader of the Opposition.

During the campaign, the Bishop-Coard teamwork, which would later lead the party to the Revolution, was very evident. Bishop, the fiery political leader with the charisma and mass appeal led the political campaign from the platform. Coard, the strategist and organiser, by then back in Grenada full-time, built and led the machinery behind the successful campaign.

In mid-1977, the final stage in the reorganisation programme was implemented. The main development was the establishment of an Organising Committee (OC). The OC was charged with the responsibility of leading and guiding the internal organisational work of the party and its work amongst the masses. Coard was the chairman of the OC, with Selwyn Strachan as his invaluable deputy. George Louison, a member of the now eight-man and much changed Political Bureau from the one which emerged from the Founding Congress, was the third Political Bureau member of the OC.

The entire party membership was also organised into 15 work committees, thereby further entrenching the principle of division of labour as a basic tenet of the party's organisational work. An Urban Workers' Committee, Farmers' Committee, Teachers' Committee, Women's Committee and Fishermen's Committee were established to undertake the party work amongst the masses. A Publications Committee was assigned all aspects of the publication work of the NJM. This committee was responsible for supervising and guiding all aspects of production and distribution of *Jewel*, the main organ of the party which was produced on a weekly basis, and five other newspapers published on a fortnightly or monthly basis. The importance the party placed on this area of work could be measured by the fact that Selwyn Strachan, then recognised in the party for his outstanding organisational ability, was placed in charge of it. An External Relations Committee, charged with developing the party's links outside Grenada, was also one of the 15 committees set up. All these committees were in turn supervised and guided by the OC.

And at the top of the NJM structure was the Political Bureau. By 1977 many of the early leaders of the NJM, including the majority of the members of the original Bureau, were no longer politically active. Some migrated. Others simply withdrew from the ranks of the party. Thus by 1977 there were eight members of the political Bureau. They were: Maurice Bishop, Unison Whiteman, Bernard Coard, Kenrick Radix, Selwyn Strachan, Hudson Austin, Vincent Noel and George Louison.

Mention should be made here of OREL (Organisation for Revolutionary Education and Liberation). OREL was a group of young intellectuals drawn from the Presentation Brothers College (PBC) and the Grenada Boys Secondary School (GBSS). Those were the two leading secondary boys' school in Grenada. At the time of its formation in 1975 some of the members of OREL had recently left school. Others were still at school. At its height the membership of OREL was approximately two dozen. But collectively they comprised a group of highly disciplined and deeply committed revolutionaries. They considered themselves professional revolutionaries willing to give anything and everything for the struggle. Members of OREL engaged in revolutionary education and studied Marxism-Leninism on a consistent basis. They engaged in education and practical work amongst youths and workers. Liam Owusu James was the leader of OREL. Among other leading members were Basil Gahagan, John Ventour and Leon Cornwall.

In the period of its existence, OREL had a very close relationship with NJM. By 1976 all OREL members were also members of NJM and actively participated in the work of the party. Several were active and, indeed, leading members of the NLA. In the 1977 reorganisation, many of them took up leading positions in the 15 work committees of the party. However, OREL continued as a separate organisation for a short while after, continuing to carry out independent work. By early 1978 OREL was disbanded as a separate organisation. The members of OREL enjoyed excellent relationships with all the leaders of the NJM. However, they were particularly close to Bernard Coard who served as a mentor to many of them.

Undoubtedly, the reorganisation of the NJM, and the full integration of the members of OREL into its ranks, gave a cutting edge to the party and transformed it into the force which would ultimately spearhead the defeat of Gairyism and led to the making of the Grenada Revolution.

*

PART C

Afterword

*

Chapter 27

'We Revolutionaries Plough the Sea'

Simon Bolivar, I read on death row, in the last days of his life allegedly said: 'We revolutionaries just plough the sea.' He was moved to this lament as he despaired at the disunity and division around him; and as he became the object of hate and spite of many of his former supporters and comrades. It seemed to him that, all that he had given his life for, all that he and his comrades had sacrificed to achieve, had come to waste.

We Grenadian revolutionaries can identify with that sentiment. Each of us in and out of prison at different moments must have felt that it was not worth it. For those who lost loved ones to the grave and/or saw their loved ones go to prison for decades, the feeling must have been very acute at times. And so it was for those of us who actually endured over two decades of imprisonment, including five years on death row.

However, I hasten to add that it is not out of any 'Bolivarian' despair that I wrote this Afterword.

177

For several years now, many of my friends have been urging me to publish this book. I resisted. Finally, I agreed to do so on the condition that I add this Afterword.

I write this Afterword out of a sense of obligation. As one who was an active participant in the making, building and (sadly) the destruction of the Grenada Revolution, I consider that if I tell the story of how it was made, I owe it to our people, and in particular the young generation and those still unborn, to put the story in the perspective of subsequent events. I therefore hope that this perspective will assist those who aspire to bring to permanent fruition the dream for which we so selflessly reached in the 1970's. In particular, I hope that it will assist them to detect potential pitfalls from an early stage and to avoid our mistakes. In this regard I am bringing to bear the wisdom and insights I have obtained through the years of solitude.

I write as one who as a young man – some may say a kid – chose the option of violent revolution. I grew up in the era of the Vietnam War, of the high point of the Cuban Revolution, when the national liberation movement was in full swing. I grew up with Che Guvera as my hero. He was my one and only revolutionary idol. His cry was for armed revolution and the violent overthrow of oppressors and their system. He died in Bolivia pursuing that cause. In my youthful years, and like many of my generation throughout the world, I saw myself as walking in the footsteps of Commandanté Che Guvera. And thus I was fully prepared to strike my blow against the Gairy dictatorship when the hour arrived.

Chapter 28

In Retrospect, Was the Revolutionary Seizure of Power Justified?

In September 1999, in an interview which was subsequently broadcast on *GBN* TV and Radio, the question was asked of me and three of my comrades: 'If it were possible to reverse the clock and take you back to March 12th 1979, would you do the same thing on March 13th?'

My answer to that question was, "Yes I would." ***Prima facie*** this was evidence that, as some said at the time, "He has not changed one bit."

But I went on to explain that by March 12th 1979 the battle lines were already drawn; it was then do or die! I could see no alternative to moving. I still can't.

However, I also went on to express the view that, with all I now know, if I were taken back to any time between 1970-1976, then I could see a different route to power and revolutionary change. I could perceive us achieving our objectives without having to resort to force of arms.

In the aforesaid interview I made reference to the experience of the late Guyanese leader, Dr. Cheddi Jagan, and his party, the PPP. It is quite remarkable that Jagan, an avowed communist, in the era of the Cold War, had the wisdom to recognise that armed struggle could lead his country to terrible tragedy. He therefore exercised exceptional patience in dealing with the Burnham government. For 28 years he was excluded from power through a series of fraudulent elections. But patiently and peacefully, he soldiered on. In the post-Cold War period his way was vindicated.

Grenada is not an exact parallel. In Guyana there was the race factor. Jagan would have realised that armed struggle would divide Guyana along race lines. In Grenada we faced no such complication. Indeed, in Grenada, power was successfully seized by force of arms. And the country was united for a period following that. It was subsequent mistakes which led to serious divisions.

I think it is correct to say, however, that from an early period, Jagan chose the path of winning power by peaceful means as a strategic option. This choice allowed his movement to exist intact for several decades while the ruling party stole election after election and mismanaged Guyana. Because of this preference for the constitutional route Jagan and his party provided no excuse for the ruling party to seek to physically eliminate or imprison Jagan and the other PPP leaders. And hence, there was little possibility that a situation of physical confrontation would be forced upon the PPP.

By comparison, I think it is correct to say that most of the young revolutionaries of the early 70's, who subsequently banded into the NJM, from the very outset were inclined to seek power by unconstitutional means. This factor, combined with the deteriorating socio-economic conditions in Grenada at the time, and the regional and international environment, made rebellion a real probability.

It is clear that no responsible government could fail to address the warning signs of rebellion. But the irony is that the way that Gairy chose to address the early signs of rebellion had the unintended consequence of fuelling the rebellion. In his famous Black Power speech in 1970, when Gairy said that "when your neighbour's house is on fire you must wet yours", he failed to make the point, or to even realise, that there was a difference between wetting a fire with water and wetting it with gasoline. By trying to use force to quell the stirrings of the Grenadian youth, Gairy spurred them on. He hardened the positions of the young revolutionaries. Initially, their preference was to march in the streets, and write Peoples' Indictments and stage Peoples' Trials. But as Gairy moved on them, they reached the point where the unconstitutional preference became a preference for armed revolution. True, Gairy had wetted his house. But he did so by throwing gasoline and diesel on a nascent fire. That fire 'greased' him and his government on March 13th 1979.

The point being made here is that if in 1970 the young revolutionaries had decided on the constitutional option as the strategic one for obtaining power, then their tactics would have been different. The confrontational style of politics would not have been practised. Gairy would not have been frightened into putting on full display the entire repertoire of his autocratic tendencies. And the NJM someday may have been able to obtain power constitutionally and then embark on its programme of socio-economic transformation. On this model the issue of moving on March 13th 1979 would, in all probability, not have arisen.

However, one must face the fact that it is quite possible that a people could face a situation where their opposition leaders conduct themselves constitutionally and democratically; that the government therefore has no excuse whatsoever to seek to move on them; but that out of a desire to hold on to power for a small clique and thereby thwart the democratic wishes of the people, the government is prepared to use force, including physical elimination of the people's leaders. In such a case it may well be that there is no alternative to the people but to rise up and throw out that government by force of arms. But even so, every conceivable alternative should be explored before taking such a grave step: for the seizure of power by unconstitutional means, and in particular by violent means, is always pregnant with immense danger, conflict and suffering.

In 1976, the NJM had tried the constitutional option by participating in the elections. However, it should be pointed out here that at the time the party was not united on the issue of participating in the elections. Indeed, the party had taken a decision not to partake in the 1976 elections. It was only after Bernard Coard returned to Grenada in September 1976, to live full time, that he was able to persuade the party to reverse itself and participate in the elections.

But Gairy stole those elections. The effect of Gairy's theft was to strengthen the tendency in the NJM which believed that the route of armed struggle to remove Gairy was the only way to go.

So by 1977 what you had in Grenada was a vibrant revolutionary organisation convinced that it would only be allowed to assume power by force, versus an autocrat bent on holding on to power by force or fraud, by any means necessary. When the inevitable flash point came, the autocrat lost.

One must accept that the seizure of power on March 13th 1979 was in keeping with the inclination of a section of the NJM leadership and with the preference of a large section of the younger revolutionaries. By this I mean that several of us were prepared to move on the dictatorship by March 13th whether or not we perceived a direct and immediate threat from Gairy. However, despite that, I still maintain that objectively the revolutionary overthrow of the Gairy dictatorship on March 13th 1979 was justified, correct and, indeed, it saved Grenada from greater misfortune.

I am clear in my mind that if the leadership of the party had decided against moving, and Gairy and his forces had succeeded in imprisoning or killing them, things would not have ended there. It is inconceivable that the younger revolutionaries would have sat idly by. Undoubtedly, we would have embarked on a course of armed resistance. Such resistance would have either ended in the forcible removal of Gairy, after much bloodshed; or in the crushing of the revolutionary forces, after much bloodshed. The decision of the leadership to move, and the pre-emptive strike by the NLA on March 13th 1979 prevented such bloodshed.

Chapter 29

The Making of the Revolution – and The Destruction of the Revolution

The view has been expressed that many of the mistakes of the Revolution had their roots in the manner in which we took power. In this regard reference has been made, in particular, to the violations of human rights which the Revolution engaged in, most notably the holding of hundreds of political detainees without charge or trial.

The line of reasoning here is that since we took power despite the law, it was very easy for us to disregard the law and disregard fundamental rights arising under the law if we deemed a political or security objective to be involved. And that in this non-rule-of-law environment it was very, very easy for people's rights to become valueless and for abuses to arise. And they did.

I subscribe to the above view. But in my opinion the issue is deeper than that. I believe that it was theoretically possible for the Revolution to come to power in the manner it did, and yet avoid the subsequent mistakes.

If the Grenada Revolution had from a very early stage opted to give full rein to all the democratic rights of the

183

people, including to those who disagreed with the Revolution, then things would have worked out differently. If we had opted for a rule of law state in which democratic elections were held and the fundamental rights of every citizen were fully and duly respected, then in my view, we would not have made the mistake of violating the rights of hundreds of our fellow citizens. And the Revolution would not have been destroyed in the tragic manner in which it finally was.

But I submit that in the historical time frame, and given realities of that period, it was not practically possible for the revolutionaries to have operated differently. That was so because the reality was that the revolutionary leadership was fundamentally immature: in 1979 the average age of the NJM CC was less than 30 years; collectively we were seriously lacking in life experience; and our basic orientation and instinct was to resolve conflicts by force. Moreover, this orientation was reinforced and stimulated by the practice of the world revolutionary movement with which the Grenada revolutionary movement merged. I honestly do not believe that the revolutionary leadership could fairly be accused of having been rigid or inflexible by nature. The management of the economy during the four and a half years and the manner in which the IMF in particular was dealt with displayed a level of flexibility which refutes any such charge of general rigidity.[54] But in the area of politics we tended to be less flexible. We considered ourselves to be Marxist-Leninist and we repeated some of the serious mistakes of the international Marxist-Leninist and revolutionary movement, particularly as regards to the approach to the issues of parliamentary democracy and respect for individual rights and freedoms.

This orientation referred to herein, to resolve conflicts by force, expressed itself in the pre-March 13th period as a preference for, or strong inclination to, armed struggle. After March 13th 1979, it pre-disposed us to use the power of the state to lock up our political opponents. Later, when some of our political opponents themselves resorted to force to resist the Revolution, we did not hesitate to use lethal force against them. Even persons who had struggled together with us to help overthrow Gairy were jailed or killed. They were not exempted. Several of the participants, including persons featured in the story of this book, were jailed. And one, Strachan Phillip, was killed in an armed assault on his house. Another revolutionary not featured in the book, but worthy of mention in this regard, was Ralph Thompson. He was renowned as one of the most selfless, courageous, and hard-working members of the NJM during the period of the anti-Gairy struggle. Week after week he faced down the feared Mongoose Gang and openly distributed hundreds of the party's newspapers in the streets of St. George. However, by the end of the first year of the Revolution he had become disillusioned, believing that he had not received the recognition that his contribution deserved. Following the attempt on the lives of the leadership on June 19th 1980, he was detained as a "counter-revolutionary", and held without charge or trial. He subsequently died in hospital as much from cancer as from a broken heart.

The criticism made here is not to put into oblivion the tremendous social and economic strides made during the years of the Revolution. Even Eric Gairy himself, on his return to Grenada after the invasion, publicly commended the social and economic achievements of the Revolution. He was forced by the reality around him to recognise that the Revolution opened up many opportunities for social and economic advancement of poor people and their children. The Revolution also made progress in involving thousands of Grenadians in the day-to-day tasks of running the country. This was in pursuance of the policy of the Revolution to broaden the process of democracy. Thousands of Grenadians who previously sat back and, at best, waited to cast their votes every five years were involved in day to day activities of the state and in governance: be it in helping to formulate the national budget; in helping to monitor the implementation of the many construction and other projects undertaken by the Revolution; in helping to organise and execute community work; in running the schools while the teachers were away undergoing teacher training; in helping to eradicate illiteracy; or through participation in the people's militia.

However, while the Revolution was prepared to involve the people and give them power over important aspects of their lives, the tendency to approach disagreements in an immature and confrontational manner, which was fed by the paranoia over the designs of the government of the United States, ran contrary to the desire to broaden the democratic process. And in the final analysis, it was the confrontational instincts – and not the democratic tendency within the Grenada Revolution (and within all the revolutionary leaders) – which prevailed.

And hence, in October 1983, when a conflict broke out within the party leadership itself, both sides to the conflict resorted to the model of conflict-resolution known to them and practised over a period of years. When faced with a challenge to his absolute leadership of the party, PM Bishop did not go to the people with the genuine issue. Instead he issued a rumour that a plan to kill him was uncovered. The other side reacted by putting PM Bishop under house arrest. From there things catapulted out of hand.

Thus on October 19th 1983, when a large crowd entered the fray and more than ever a conciliatory approach was needed, one side headed for Fort Rupert while the other side headed for Fort Frederick. One side had the people with them; and they were convinced they were right because 'the voice of the masses is the voice of God.' The other side – the Central Committee Majority – had principle, the party masses and the military on their side, and they too were convinced they were right because 'principle is principle'.

The truth is, neither side could have won. It was a lose-lose situation. A compromise alone could have provided winners. But we were not skilled in the art of compromise. It was not part of our arsenal. At that tense moment when

186

everything was balanced on a knife edge, we had no experience of compromise, negotiations, or of serious give and take, and some-for-you-some-for-me thinking, to fall back on. Our years as a movement were one of solving conflicts by confrontation or force; by 'heavy manners': that was our reflex action. That experience finally caught up with us.

And so both sides squared off. And at that moment it became inevitable: one side or the other would meet their demise. It was a Greek tragedy.

I mentioned above that Che Guvera was my hero. I still admire many things about Che: his concern for people; his willingness and capacity for sacrifice in order to assist others, in particular the poor and oppressed; and his humility. But I renounce the thinking and methods of the 1970's. I still abhor oppression and exploitation; but I do not believe that there is any short-term solution to those. Nor do I believe that the prescriptions of the world revolutionary movement of the 1950's-80's could solve the problems of poverty, powerlessness and oppression. In many cases, the revolutionary movements bred as much oppression as they set out to solve.

I now hold the view that the way forward for those who set out to develop the nation and to achieve a better way of life for the people is through:

1.   The generation of opportunities for people to uplift themselves academically, materially, culturally and spiritually;

2.   A full scale democratic process, drawing the entire populace into the process of governance; and

3.   The uncompromising respect for civil rights, human rights and human dignity.

All three must be pursued simultaneously.

It may sound ironic that someone who was a leading player in a process that engaged in the suppression and violation of civil and human rights of a section of the population, should now be taking the position I take herein. But this position was arrived at through great reflection over many years and in the context of my own suffering. It was so very easy to hate and desire revenge. The same type of hate which has plunged many nations into a vicious cycle of violence with yesterday's victims becoming tomorrow's oppressors. And, in the early years of incarceration, I did hate and prayed for revenge.

However, as the years went by the hatred and the desire for revenge melted and I recognised that there is a lofty road, that of forgiveness and reconciliation. I realised that I needed forgiveness and had to myself forgive.

In this process I was greatly assisted by events in South Africa. Like all my colleagues, I was moved by the example of the South African revolutionaries led by the great Nelson Mandela. After 27 years of incarceration that great man walked out of prison devoid of bitterness and willing to sit down and work out things with his oppressors for the good of humanity and for the good of his country.

By then, however, I was able to understand just how that was possible. I myself had direct experience of a remarkable Grenadian. Mr Winston Courtney was the Commissioner at the Richmond Hill Prisons from 1991-1996. He was one of yesterday's victims. Prior to the Grenada Revolution he was a senior police officer. Indeed, at one time he was head of the intelligence arm of the police. To that extent one can say that he was a part of the oppressor system. During the Revolution he was arrested and detained without charge or trial. He became a victim. While in prison, his eldest son was killed by opponents of the Revolution in quite bizarre circumstances. As a result, he was allowed to attend his son's funeral and thereafter released and permitted to leave the country. In the aftermath of his imprisonment and his son's death he lost everything. He even lost his family, which crumbled under the enormous strain and stress. He therefore had every reason to hate us.

Once Mr Courtney took up a senior position at the prison the expectation was that he would exact revenge and we braced ourselves for that. Instead, over a period of six years that man treated us with a level of humanity which simply humbled me and brought me face to face with my maker. That was a lesson to me. A lesson that our world is not made up of exploiters and exploited, oppressors and oppressed, working class and capitalist; our society is not made up of philosophical categories. Our society is made up of people; of human beings. I came to realise that if one could see beyond the categories and formulae, beyond the collective descriptions, and reach out to the human being, so much is possible. And I recognised, in a more profound way than ever before, that with all our imperfections, humanity is still God's greatest creation and should be so treated.

It is against the background of all the above, I say to our young people that:

1. Armed struggle viewed as a preference for solving political problems, is politically immature and in my view morally wrong;

2. It is possible for a people to pursue their aspirations for a better life and to change society so that there are more opportunities for more, and more equitable distribution of society's fruits, through legal and constitutional means. I believe that the experiment now on the way next door in Venezuela may well provide strong evidence of this;

3. However, there are exceptional circumstances when it is legitimate for a people to utilise armed struggle as a necessary means to rid themselves of their oppressors and to

herald a period of change. Such exceptional circumstances must be truly exceptional. There must be no other way to get rid of the oppressors; and the suffering, chaos and dislocation arising from the use of armed struggle must not outweigh that resulting from the conduct of the oppressors;

4. If power is assumed by way of armed struggle or by unconstitutional means, the responsibility falls on those who take power in the name of the people to quickly return the country to a rule of law mode. The law is a powerful instrument of social engineering that can then be used in pursuit of the desired changes. This I think is the experience thus far of Hugo Chavez in Venezuela today. And this was definitely the experience of the American revolutionaries who brought the USA into existence in the late 18th century.

5. Finally, drawing on my own experience and that of most of my colleagues imprisoned with me, I would urge our youth to use their youthful years to concentrate on educating and equipping themselves for their future roles in society. It's definitely a positive thing to develop and nurture a social conscience from an early age. But deep involvement in politics can and should wait until you are more mature and have gained a wide life-experience.

Chapter 30

Post Prison Reflections

On 5th September 2009, I was finally released from prison. The foregoing parts of this Afterword were written in 1999; in prison. Outside of grammatical adjustments, I have not changed any of it.

The society I was released into is a much changed one from that I left in 1983. Technologically, it is a different world. Before going to prison I had not seen a computer and the Internet was a decade away. Additionally, Grenada is now a society dominated by women. This advancement of women is in my view the most significant social development in the last 30 years. It is my expectation that this role will be further enhanced in coming decades.

I still consider the US invasion of 1983 to have been illegal and unwarranted. I believe that post 19th October 1983, Grenadians, with the help of our Caribbean neighbours and other Commonwealth nations, could and would have found a solution to our problems; a solution that would have fully restored constitutional rule and the all the rights of our people in a reasonably short time; and would have provided justice according to law rather than according to political imperatives and expediency: This would have been achieved without the loss of scores of Grenadian lives and additional trauma which flowed from the invasion. Events which took place in Eastern Europe in the years shortly after the demise of the Grenada Revolution strengthen my belief in this regard.

However, I do accept that there have been important democratic gains since 1983. Significantly, Grenadians have been able to change their government through the ballot box on four occasions since then. This right to choose and change a nation's government through the ballot box is a sacred right. The perception and reality that Grenadians were being denied that right during the Gairy period was one of the main reasons for the 1979 Revolution. If Grenadians guard this right jealously and zealously by ensuring that there is no corruption of it through administrative and other means, and that the process is always subjected to the greatest possible scrutiny, then we should be guaranteed steady evolutionary change.

Another democratic gain has been in the area of freedom of expression. The competition between the many print and electronic media houses and the emergence of the internet has made for robust public discourse on a range of political and social issues.

Unfortunately, though, the experience of the village and zonal councils from the revolutionary period where the people exercised a form of direct democracy has been eschewed by subsequent governments. Many of the revolutionary economic policies of the period 1979-1983 such as the development of a vibrant agro-industrial sector have been also eschewed.

However, successive governments since 1983 have had to rely on many persons who were educated, or rose to leadership, during the revolutionary period to man the state machinery. Additionally persons from the revolutionary period can be found in every field of national endeavour making positive contributions.

Overall, I believe that in the eyes of Grenadians the Revolution has a mixed balance sheet. On the credit side are the enormous social and economic gains of the period and the sense of nationalism and national pride that it inspired. On the debit side are the violations of rights experienced by some nationals and the bloody events of October 1983. Of course there are those who, for their own reasons, are bent solely on propagandizing about the Revolution. To them there were no credits; nothing was remotely good about that process. I am confident that such persons represent only a tiny minority of Grenadians and moreover much of such garbage actually emanate from outside of Grenada. But the majority of Grenadians, 70 % of whom were born after 1983, are ready to embrace our history as Grenada's history. To celebrate the good and be knowledgeable of the bad in full awareness that good and bad often go together in great human endeavours.

Finally, I am grateful for the way wide cross sections of Grenadians have accepted me and my colleagues back in society. Given the mountain of negative propaganda that was unleashed against us by the US Psychological Operations battalion, which formed part of the invasion force, and perpetuated for decades after, it was easy to believe that none of us would ever be able to walk the streets of Grenada and more so to live in Grenada. And many outside of Grenada believed that. However, I was always confident that the propaganda which painted us as evil, vicious, blood thirsty criminals, power hungry crazy men and so on was so out of touch with reality that it would not stand.

However, I do recognize that though our country has come a long way since 1983 in terms of healing, many Grenadians are still hurting. The inability to recover the remains of the late Prime Minister Bishop is still a sore point to which the answer, I am absolutely sure, does not lie with any of my colleagues. In all probability, a conclusive answer to that mystery lies in an office in Washington DC.

*

BIBLIOGRAPHY

1. BERNARD, Callistus, They Can Only Kill Me Once, Hibiscus Publications, London, 2007

2. BRIZAN, George, **Grenada: Island of Conflict: From Amerindians to People's Revolution, 1498-1979**, Zed Books Ltd., London, 1984 Edition.

3. COARD, Bernard, **The Role Of The State In Agriculture**, University of Guyana/ IDS/ISER, 1978

4. COARD, Bernard, **Grenada: 1951-1983,** mimeo, 2003.

5. EMMANUEL, Patrick, **Crown Colony Politics In Grenada, 1917-1951**, Occasional Paper No. 7, Institute of Social and Economic Research, U.W.I, Cave Hill, Barbados, 1978.

6. FRANKLIN, Omowale, **Two Grenadas, Talented House Publications (1999).**

7. GAIRY, Eric Mathew, **Black Power In Grenada Speech**, Government Printing Office, St. George, Grenada, 1970.

8. KNIGHT, E. Gittens (compiler) **The Grenada Handbook And Directory 1946,** 1st Edition, Barbados Advocate, Barbados, 1946.

9. HOLNESS, Chris, 'The Present Political Situation In Grenada', Socialism, Vol. 2, No. 1, Kingston, Jamaica, 1975

10. MARTIN, John Angus, **Island Caribs and French Settlers in Grenada,** Grenada National Museum Press St. George's Grenada, 2013

11. SMITH, MG., 'Structure and Crisis in Grenada, 1950-1954', in MG Smith's **The Plural Society In The**

British West Indies, University of California Press, Berkeley and Los Angeles, 1965.

12. SMITH, M.G., **Stratification In Grenada**, University of California Press, Berkeley and Los Angeles, 1965.

13. SINGHAM, A.W., **The Hero And The Crowd In A Colonial Polity**, Yale university press, New Heven London, 1968.

14. **REPORT Of The Commission Of Inquiry Into The Control Of Public Expenditure In Grenada During 1961 'and subsequently'**, Government Printer, St. George's, Grenada, 1962 [the so-called "Squandamania" Report]

15. DUFFUS COMMISSION Report, **Commission of Inquiry into the Breakdown Of Law and Order, and Police Brutality In Grenada, 1974**; 27th February 1975, Kingston, Jamaica, and St. George Grenada.

16. COLONIAL OFFICE, **A Note On Grenada Disturbances, February-March 1951, Colonial Office Grenada Document, 1951**.

17. **The New Jewel** newspaper: weekly issues from March 1973 to March 1979.

18. **Manifesto of the New Jewel Movement**, 4th November 1973.

NOTES

[1] Up until then Grenada had been a colony of Britain

[2] See pages163-167.

[3] See page 34 for more details of fraudulent allegations related to the elections.

[4] See pages 172-173 for more on OREL.

[5] See pages 171-172 on how the NJM was reorganized in 1977.

[6] See page 166.

[7] Less than one month after the 1976 parliamentary elections Bishop, Coard and Whiteman spearheaded a demonstration in the villages of St. Paul's and La Borie to protest an act of police brutality over the New Year Holiday. Gairy responded to this exercise by the people of their constitutional right to peaceful protest by sending in soldiers and armed police to mash up the protest. There was a tense stand-off between the demonstrators and the soldiers and police. The situation was however defused by the intervention of a senior police officer, Superintendent Lucky Bernard, who ordered the soldiers and police to back-off and allow the demonstrators to march quietly and in peace. Shortly after that day Superintendent Bernard was removed from his position of command.

[8] See pages 37-38 for a description of the 19th June 1977 event.

[9] The Commission of Inquiry was set up on December 6th 1973, prior to independence, but most of its hearings took place after independence was attained on February 7th 1974. See George Brizan (1984), pp 343-345 for more on the circumstances in which the Commission was set up, the scope of its inquiry and some of its conclusions.

[10] Conrad Mayers was killed on 19th October 1983 while commanding the military unit which was dispatched to recapture

the army headquarters after it was seized by a crowd led by Prime Minister Bishop.

[11] Crapaud is a toad common in Grenada. It is frequently caught and killed by children.

[12] Noel was a member of the Political Bureau at the time. He was also the President of the Bank and General Workers Union (BGWU). He died tragically at Fort Rupert on October 19th 1983.

[13] Many of the allegations herein of electoral fraud were contained in affidavits filed in court in legal challenges to the 1976 election results.

[14] Gairy sent two of his top officers to receive military training there, and received arms shipments also from General Pinochet

[15] In the 1970's environment, the term terrorism did not connote the targeting of large numbers of innocent civilians as the term came to connote later, especially in the aftermath of the attack in New York on September 11th 2001. As explained in the text, within the NJM, the term connoted the use of individual acts of violence targeted at leading figures of the regime (though not ruling out collateral damage) in the belief that such acts of violence were sufficient to bring down the dictatorship.

[16] The author was at the time a secondary school teacher of mathematics and economics.

[17] Some former officials of Gairy government have denied that any such instructions were given. They also deny that there was any intention to kill or otherwise use violence against the NJM leaders in November 1978 as stated in this book. I would readily admit that to the best of my information, NJM did not possess evidence of such orders or intention by Gairy which was admissible in a court of law. However, that is not the issue. I respectfully submit that the issue was whether there were reasonable grounds for the NJM leaders to believe that Gairy was coming for them and whether they honestly so believed. The events outlined in this book provide ample grounds for the NJM leaders to believe that Gairy was coming for them. And based on my own observations which I seek to convey in this book, it was absolutely clear that the NJM leaders were convinced that they were in real and present danger.

[18] The mention of cells resonated due to the fact that it was known that a total of eight cells had been constructed in an underground section at the Richmond Hill Prisons somewhere around 1976. It was public knowledge that there were eight members of the NJM leadership and the popular perception and view within the NJM was that these cells were built for the NJM leaders.

[19] See Martin, John Angus (2013) pp 54-77 for a more detail treatment of the conflict between the French colonizers and the Caribs for control of Grenada.

[20] Originally the main term used to describe the leadership was "the Bureau". However, the term Political Bureau was also used. After the Revolution with the formation of the Central Committee as the executive of the party the term "Political Bureau" became entrenched. The term Political Bureau will therefore be used throughout this text. (After the Revolution members of the Political were selected from the membership of the Central Committee.)

[21] **George Brizan** (1984), pp 241-251, characterizes the social upheavals of 1951 as a Social Revolution. **Brizan** (1984), Page 249, points out that the Governor and the British official sent into Grenada to mediate viewed the events as more than a labour dispute. They recognized that a revolution was underway in Grenada. The author fully accepts the characterization of the 1951 upheavals as a Social Revolution. They had all the hallmarks of a social revolution. They involved the mass mobilization of an oppressed class (agricultural workers and poor peasants) to challenge the power of the ruling class (the plantocracy) with the aim of breaking the power of the old rulers and installing their representatives as the rulers of Grenada. Of course 1951 did not spell the end of the power of the planters in Grenada. But it marked the beginning of the end of planter power.

[22] For students interested in studying Grenada's social structure in the pre-Gairy and early-Gairy periods, there is no better place to start than the two works by M.G. Smith listed in the bibliography. The seminal work on Grenada's political and constitutional history, political sociology, and political economy (up to the early 1960's) is **A.W. Singham's** 1968 work (listed, also, in the bibliography, as are all references to works by various authors in these footnotes). For a detailed examination of Grenada's politics in the thirty-year

period immediately before Eric Gairy's arrival on Grenada's political scene, and for his brief analysis of the 1951 revolution, **Pat Emmanuel's** 1978 work is recommended. **George Brizan's** 1984 work (chapters 16 and 17) is recommended for an understanding of the growth of the peasantry and of the trade union movement in Grenada. His panoramic view of Grenada's constitutional and political history: "From Crown Colony rule to Revolution" (chapter 20) is also recommended. **Chris Holness'** 1975 paper brings the analysis of Grenada's sociological, political and economic changes up to the birth of NJM and indeed up to its first major political battle: the 1973-1974 "crisis" and "defeat". Finally, **B. Coard's** brief mimeograph (2003) summarizes the political and constitutional developments of the turbulent 33-year period, 1951-1983.

[23] For one fascinating (sociological) perspective on the cause of the crisis (and "revolution") in 1951, see **M.G. Smith's (1965)** 'Structure and Crisis in Grenada'. For a somewhat different (political scientist's) viewpoint, see **A.W. Singham (1968)**, especially pages 145-169. For the outlook of a Grenadian historian and economist see **G. Brizan (1984)**, pages 226-264. Finally, for yet another viewpoint, see **C. Holness (1975)**.

[24] **C. Holness (1975)**; **A.W. Singham (1968)**, pp 36-41; **P. Emmanuel (1978)**, pp 144-157; **G. Brizan (1984)** page 254-264, 271.

[25] P. Emmanuel (1978), pp 158-165; C. Holness (1975), G. Brizan (1984), pages 254-264.

[26] P. Emmanuel (1978), pp 176-185; G. Brizan (1984) pp 241-251; A.W. Singham (1968), pp 145-169.

[27] **C. Holness (1975)**; **P. Emmanuel (1978)**, page 178, especially the footnote on the page containing the police report on the violence and destruction of property; **Colonial Office (1951)**, giving great details on the disturbances; **A. W. Singham (1968)** pp 161-167. This includes a ministerial statement in the House of Commons in England on the disturbances (see footnote #23 on pages 161-162); G. Brizan (1984).

[28] C. Holness (1975); A.W. Singham (1968) pp 161-167; G. Brizan (1984) 242-246; Colonial Office (1951).

---

[29] Colonial Office (1951), C. Holness (1975); A. W. Singham (1968) page 167, G. Brizan (1984) page 249.

[30] P. Emmanuel (1978), pp 178-179; G. Brizan (1984) pp 242-251; A. W. Singham (1968) page 169; C. Holness (1975), B. Coard (2003).

[31] Despite popular belief in Grenada, adult suffrage in Grenada was not a direct consequence of the 1951 Revolution. The decision to institute universal adult suffrage preceded the 1951 Revolution. See A.W. Singham (1968) pp 111-117, 170; G. Brizan (1984), pp 318-319.

[32] **A. W. Singham (1968)** pp 99-144, especially pp 117-120.

[33] C. Holness (1975), B. Coard (1978), A. W. Singham (1968), pp 56-61.

[34] **B. Coard (1978)** gives a detailed breakdown of all the agricultural estates which Gairy seized from his political foes under the compulsory acquisition law, and discusses the uses to which they were put.

[35] A. W. Singham (1968) pp 194-195;

[36] A. W. Singham (1968) especially pp 169-171, G. Brizan (1984), C. Holness (1975). P. Emmanuel (1978).

[37] Appendix 3 of **G. Brizan (1984)** provides detailed election results for all general elections from 1951 to 1976 inclusive: pp 359 et. seq. See also pages 328-329.

[38] Report of the Commission of Enquiry (1962); A. W. Singham (1968) pp 207- 209, 234-240, and pp 245-249; G. Brizan (1984) pp 321-325.

[39] G. Brizan (1984) pp 327-328.

[40] See issues of **The New Jewel** (weekly) for the period March 1973 to March 1979 for details on all of this. See also **The Manifesto of the New Jewel Movement**, November 4th, 1973. Also **C. Holness (1975)**.

[41] G. Brizan (1984) (pp 323- 325) provides the details of the 17 debt cases: the amounts owed, to whom, and the year in which action was filed in the High Court to recover the debts owed by Gairy to these persons and businesses.

[42] In 1979 Gairy owned **Rock Gardens, Evening Palace**, and **Tropical Inn** – all small hotels with bars, etc; and he was reputedly the part owner of **Hamilton Inn** and **Spice Island Inn**. He also owned several acres of land in the Golf Course area, among other properties.

[43] Duffus Commission Report (1975). See also Brizan (1984) pp 329-332.

[44] **Grenada Census** data for 1960, 1970, and 1980 capture this phenomenon in detail.

[45] Brizan (1984) pp 283-295 gives data on the expansion of educational opportunities for that period inter alia

[46] **Grenada Census**, 1970 and 1980; also **Coard (78)**.

[47] See issues of **The New Jewel** (weekly) for the period March 1973 to March 1979; **G. Brizan (1984)** pp 330-331.

[48] Eric Gairy (1970).

[49] For details on the scale of state-sponsored brutality under Gairy, the best source of concrete evidence is the **Duffus Commission Report (1975)**; also issues of **The New Jewel** for the period March 1973-March 1979.

[50] There was no system of ID cards, or the staining of fingers upon casting one's vote. [These were not introduced until the December 1984 elections!]. Moreover, literally thousands of individuals were registered to vote in several polling divisions, and even in more than one constituency. There was therefore no effective way of preventing multiple voting – or vote – impersonation (including even dead people 'resurrecting' and voting, before returning to their graves!). The 1972 and 1976 elections gained their notoriety as a result of the above electoral deficiencies and malpractices.

[51] See **The New Jewel** (weekly), for the period March 1973 to February 1974; also **The Manifesto of The New Jewel Movement,** November 4th, 1973.

[52] **The Manifesto of The New Jewel Movement,** November 4th, 1973. The document comprised 10,000 words, covering all aspects

of the NJM's proposed programme for Grenada's social, political and economic transformation.

[53] **The Duffus Commission Report (1975)** provides detailed testimony and other evidence regarding the "Bloody Sunday" incident, and the handling of it by the magistrate and other public officials.

[54] The IMF provided millions of dollars in loans to Grenada during the Revolution without unacceptable or onerous conditions being attached; and in its 1982 Annual Report the World Bank praised the management of the economy.

17707729R00125

Made in the USA
Middletown, DE
05 February 2015